THREE MODEL THEATRES

Elizabethan theatre

THREE
MODEL THEATRES

━━━━━━━

ELIZABETHAN

EIGHTEENTH CENTURY

MODERN

━━━━━━━

ROY SMITH

THOMAS NELSON AND SONS LTD
EDINBURGH

THOMAS NELSON AND SONS LTD
Parkside Works Edinburgh 9
36 Park Street London W1
312 Flinders Street Melbourne C1

302–304 Barclays Bank Building
Commissioner and Kruis Streets
Johannesburg

THOMAS NELSON AND SONS (CANADA) LTD
91–93 Wellington Street West   Toronto 1

THOMAS NELSON AND SONS
19 East 47th Street New York 17

SOCIÉTÉ FRANÇAISE D'ÉDITIONS NELSON
97 rue Monge Paris 5

———

Printed in Great Britain by
Thomas Nelson and Sons Ltd, Edinburgh

CONTENTS

v

LIST OF PLATES

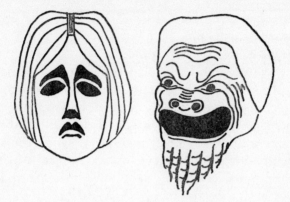

INTRODUCTION

This is a book of instructions on how to build for
yourself a model theatre—or, rather, three theatres
of different times—for a fairly small amount of
money. It is not a book only for experienced
model-makers : even if you've never made a model
in your life you don't have to feel uneasy. Every
step is explained fully and simply, and you should
have no difficulty in following exactly what to do.
However, here I must warn you that as a theatre
is a complicated sort of building the making of a
model of one is not something that can be done
in an evening. It will take time and care, and you
may at times lose patience and feel like giving up.
But once it—or they—is finished you will realise
it was worth it. A model theatre can give you
hours of enjoyment and fascination : you can

I

make and cut out furniture, sets, figures or characters, and put on plays of all kinds. Some people
write their own plays for model theatres and some
even make lighting equipment.

The three models in this book are not copies in
miniature of buildings that exist or once existed,
but are based on the kind of design for theatres
in the time of Queen Elizabeth I, in the eighteenth
century and at the present day. It would be very
difficult indeed to build an exact replica of a real
theatre, and so complicated and intricate that it
would cost a lot of money, take a long time, and
prove in the end to be delightful to look at but
useless to play around with.

Since there are three theatres of different times
in this book, and as some of you may be interested
in how the theatres changed in the West from very
early times to the present, the next section is about
their development over many centuries.

A VERY SHORT HISTORY
OF THE THEATRE

The earliest theatres of which we have any real
knowledge are those of Ancient Greece—about
2,400 years ago. No-one knows why, when or
how, the performing of plays began, although it
is generally thought that they developed from
religious songs and dances. However, the following
story is a possibility.

In Greece there was once a very famous actor called Thespis who travelled round the countryside giving performances from a cart—a movable stage in fact. One day in Athens he and his company drew such crowds and caused such a jam in the market-place that the authorities ordered them to leave and find some other place where they wouldn't interfere with the traffic. At the bottom of the hillside below the Acropolis stood a temple dedicated to the god of wine, Dionysos, and in front of this building, on a round, cleared space of earth, the actors found a place to perform. This space—called an orchestra by the Greeks—may have been used before for songs and dances in honour of the god, but it was a good choice in any case because the temple provided an interesting background and the audience could sit on the slope of the hill and look down on the performers.

Later on—here and in other places—the slope was scooped out or built up into a great semi-circle with stone seats rising in tiers. Then, facing the audience on the far side of the orchestra, a special building called a skene was erected : it had a long front wall with columns and, possibly, doorways, and was used by the actors as a set or scene and as a convenient place to change behind. Sometimes a raised platform ran along the front of the skene wall—perhaps for some of the performers to stand on—and this addition was given the name of proskenion, a name, in the form of proscenium, still used in theatres today (Fig. a).

Some forms of scenery were undoubtedly used, such as movable screens with pictures painted on them, three-sided flats which revolved on a pivot to show three different scenes, and even flying-machines for bringing down the gods from heaven. In these theatres both tragedies and comedies were performed ; the actors wore exaggerated masks to

Fig. a

hide their own faces and play different characters, while dignified clothes and high-soled and -heeled shoes were used in tragedy, and tights with very short jerkins in comedy.

The Romans copied the design of the Greek theatre, as they copied many Greek forms of art, but they made alterations and additions. Often the seating area was joined to the stage building so that the theatre was entirely walled in, while the stage building was extended right across the semi-circle and sometimes raised to four or five storeys in height. The circular orchestra, used by the choruses of dancers and singers in the Greek plays, was reduced to a semi-circle; and sometimes a trench was dug into which a curtain for screening the stage, could be lowered. Above the proscenium was erected a large roof (Fig. b).

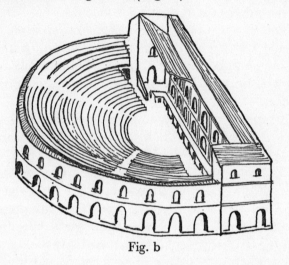

Fig. b

The theatre is now beginning to look more familiar : a stage and auditorium in the one building, a roof (even if only covering part of the stage), a large raised platform definitely used by the actors, and a curtain which could shut off the stage from the audience.

It seems, however, that the Romans were not as interested in tragedies as the Greeks. Comedies were more popular and the theatres often put on shows which were more like circuses than real plays. Fights with gladiators, wild beasts and condemned prisoners, not the dramatised stories of Hercules and the heroes of the Trojan War, began to draw vast crowds of spectators.

With the collapse of Roman power and the disapproval by the increasing number of Christians of play-acting the theatres fell into disuse. Perhaps the actors and their descendants, scattered all over Europe, carried on their art in the form of miming, dancing, acrobatics and minstrelsy, but for hundreds of years, during the Dark Ages, there is little trace of them.

Strangely enough acting and playwriting began again through the Christian church—began indeed inside the church itself. About 900 years ago stories from the Bible were performed by priests in front of the congregations—episodes such as the discovery that the body of Jesus had disappeared from the sepulchre. These little plays became so popular that in order to give everybody a chance of seeing them they were performed outside the church on the great steps leading to the West door. As time went on stories with devils and comic characters were added to the serious ones, and people came to laugh and be entertained, not to be taught or uplifted in spirit. Perhaps the church didn't approve of all this for eventually the priests had to give up acting themselves and ordinary people took over their parts. To reach a bigger audience—or because they were ordered away—

6

Fig. c

the amateur actors left the front of the church and moved into the streets and market-places.

In England—about 600 years ago—the plays were performed on certain holidays by members of trade groups or guilds, each guild being responsible for one play-episode in a series (the Shipwrights put on the story of Noah and the Ark). But as yet there was no permanent building to act in. These plays were performed in temporary booths or on large carts that could be drawn from place to place. Scenery was built to represent various settings such as the Garden of Eden, the Inn at Bethlehem and the Mouth of Hell (Fig. c).

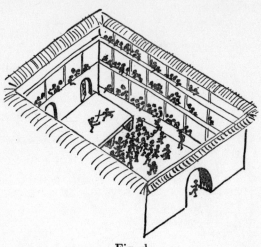

Fig. d

Plays and pageants continued to be performed in private halls, gardens, and temporary theatres set up in the streets on special occasions (the entry of a monarch into a town), but it was not until about 1575 that a permanent building for acting was erected. Before this the best place for a make-shift theatre was probably the yard of an inn, the platform stage put up against the wall opposite the entrance and the spectators standing on the ground or seated in the galleries which ran along the two side walls (Fig. d).

The first theatre building probably looked much like this, and the others that followed had roughly the same design—the large platform projecting out over the floor, two doors behind for exits and entrances, and a gallery above for musicians or for

8   (2,238)

another acting area on a higher level. To these were added, in the back walk between the two doors, a recess which could be curtained off, two windows flanking the gallery, a second gallery above that, and finally a roof supported by two great columns sheltering the stage itself. The whole building could be rectangular, octangular or even round. This is the kind of theatre which you can build a model of from the first set of instructions in this book—the Elizabethan playhouse.

For much of the seventeenth century the fear of plague, the disapproval of the Puritans and the Civil War held up play-going and therefore theatre-building. It was not until the end of the century that it began again ; the first Restoration theatre being a converted tennis court. New ideas, many from Italy and France, led to a change of design. In the Elizabethan playhouse there had been little scenery and little artificial lighting, but in the Restoration theatres these became very important. The buildings were roofed in ; the large projecting part of the stage was reduced in size, and the area behind the curtain increased ; and seats were provided on the floor. Perspective was used in set design, often with great ingenuity—so that a stage ten yards deep might give the impression of ten hundred yards. At first, indeed, the pictorial effect was of such interest that all the acting took place on the projecting area or apron-stage leaving the up-stage space for magnificent vistas. Most of this scenery consisted of painted flats—large rectangular wooden frames covered with canvas—which moved in grooves cut into the stage floor. They were often placed in pairs, one behind the other, and when one set was pulled away into the wings another set was ready with a different scene. The two doors of the Elizabethan theatre remained in front of the curtain and so did the windows above. Some of the audience watched the plays from these windows or boxes while others even sat on the stage itself down at the sides in the front. During the eighteenth century the design remained much the same although the spectators on the stage and above the doors eventually disappeared—reluctantly.

A theatre of this time is the second model which can be constructed from this book.

Increase in size was the main development of theatres in the nineteenth century : one member of the audience once complained that he could not see the faces of the actors ' without the aid of a pocket telescope '. One innovation was the use of gas for lighting. This had previously been done by candle chandeliers and by footlights of wicks floating in oil (the expression ' floats ' is still used). Scenery and spectacular effects became more and more important—as did the acting area behind the curtain—and this led eventually to the actors being, as it were, cut off from the audience by the proscenium arch. The grooves in the stage floor disappeared and instead the flats ran along, and were supported by, bars or upper grooves fixed or suspended above the stage (Fig. e).

The modern theatre is in some ways simpler than the Victorian. It is usually smaller and less elaborate in decoration; the flats no longer run in grooves, but are held upright in any position wanted on the stage by supports or braces at the

Fig. e

back; and much of the scenery can be raised from or lowered on to the stage from ropes and pulleys high up in the ceiling (the pulleys are fixed at an area known as the grid, and the ropes are worked from the flies). Lighting by electricity is often complicated and ingenious and can be used to gain many wonderful effects. It is true that there are other devices and other machines that can add to quick changes of scene, such as revolving stages,

11

and stages which have sections of their floors able to rise to any desired height, but these are not common.

The third model in this book is of a typical modern theatre.

A NOTE ON MATERIALS
AND CONSTRUCTION

The three models in this book are all built on the same basic principle : sections of wood fixed to one another by pins. This means that each theatre can be dismantled and reassembled in a few minutes. When you wish to store your model or models away somewhere, you need only a small space—for the various parts can be stacked flat, one on top or by the side of the other.

Wood is used in preference to cardboard for two reasons : one, it is very difficult to pin a piece of cardboard to another piece ; two, cardboard is inclined to bend or crack under strain. There is, of course, a third reason—a model made of wood will last much longer and will be much firmer.

Glue is used only for a few minor constructions.

The material necessary for the bases and outside walls of the models is hard-wood, $1''$ and $\frac{1}{2}''$ thick. This gives each theatre a really solid framework capable of taking rough treatment without damage. You may have to buy this hard-wood, but it is much more likely that you will be able to find enough of it from old boxes, crates or planks that nobody wants any more.

The interior walls and floors are made mainly from plywood. This you are not likely to find lying about. Buy good-quality plywood if you can—especially for the stage floors where it is most important.

The other kind of wood used, particularly in the Modern Theatre, is lath-wood $\frac{7}{8}''$ in width and $\frac{3}{16}''$ thick. This, again, you may find unwanted—from old trellis work or from the walls of a demolished building.

Don't worry if the only wood you can find is rough or dirty or damaged ; you can hide the defects easily enough with paint. Before each set of instructions is a list of the amount of each material required with its approximate price ($1''$ and $\frac{1}{2}''$ hard-wood prices are not included because you shouldn't have to buy them) together with a list of tools necessary for the job.

The following is a price-list of the materials used in the construction of the three models :

$1''$ Hard-wood	
$\frac{1}{2}''$ Hard-wood	
Ordinary plywood	7d to 9d per sq. ft.
Mahogany-finished plywood	1s 3d to 1s 6d per sq. ft.
$\frac{7}{8}''$ ($1''$) Lath-wood	1d to 2d per foot
$\frac{3}{4}''$ Dowell-rod	4d per foot
Thick wire	1s 5d per lb.
	(20 yds. approx.)

1″ Oval nails	1s 9d per lb.
¾″ Veneer/panel pins	2s 11d per lb.
½″ Staples	2s 1d per lb.
Small screw-eyes	3½d per dozen
Glue	1s to 1s 3d per tube

Paint, thread, cotton reels, drawing-pins, cardboard, tin.

Where prices are not mentioned I have assumed that you will have these things at home.

Materials required :

		from
Plywood	9 sq. ft.	6s 7d to 8s 3d
$\frac{1}{2}$″ Hard-wood	4 sq. ft.	
1″ Hard-wood	3 sq. in.	
$\frac{7}{8}$″ Lath-wood	3 ft.	3d to 6d
$\frac{3}{4}$″ Dowelling	13 in.	6d
Cotton reels	2	
Tin sheet	$4\frac{1}{2}$ sq. in.	
1″ Oval nails	2 oz.	3d
$\frac{3}{4}$″ Veneer-pins	1-oz. packet	6d
Glue	1 tube	1s 3d
Paint (Emulsion/Oil)	$\frac{1}{4}$ pint	
Paint (Poster)	2 small jars	

Total   from 9s 4d to 11s 3d

Tools required :

Hammer, saw (for hard-wood), tenon-saw (for plywood), wire-cutters, pliers, ruler (with $\frac{1}{8}$s and $\frac{1}{16}$s), pencil, set-square or triangle, protractor, sandpaper, knife or razor blade. (Additional tools— not essential : shooting-board, plane, fret-saw, chisel, spike, spirit-level.)

The base and back walls of the model of the Elizabethan Theatre are best made of wood about $\frac{1}{2}''$ thick. You should be able to find pieces suitable from old boxes or crates easily enough. First of all you will need a rectangular piece, $17\frac{1}{2}''$ by $16\frac{1}{4}''$ —and this will be the base upon which the model stands.

Then measure off two lengths, $14\frac{1}{2}''$ by $1\frac{1}{2}''$, and another two, $13\frac{3}{4}''$ by $1\frac{1}{2}''$.

When you have sawn off these five sections, take a piece of fairly coarse sandpaper and rub off all the furry edges caused by the action of the saw.

Lay the base piece on a table, bench or floor : along the sides measuring $16\frac{1}{4}''$ draw two lines parallel to the edges and $1\frac{1}{2}''$ in from the edges ; draw another line parallel to one of the $17\frac{1}{2}''$ sides and $\frac{7}{8}''$ in ; and another parallel to the other $17\frac{1}{2}''$ side and $\frac{5}{8}''$ in. Within the rectangular base you will now have another rectangle measuring $14\frac{3}{4}''$ by $14\frac{1}{2}''$. Turn the base section so that the line $\frac{5}{8}''$ in from the side is nearest to you and mark that line ' a ', the line opposite it ' b ', the line to your left ' c ', and the remaining line ' d '. (See Fig. 1.)

Your $14\frac{1}{2}''$ by $1\frac{1}{2}''$ pieces will stand along lines ' a ' and ' b ', and the $13\frac{3}{4}''$ by $1\frac{1}{2}''$ pieces along lines ' c ' and ' d '.

Take one of the $14\frac{1}{2}''$ by $1\frac{1}{2}''$ lengths and stand it on one of its long edges. Place an $1''$ oval nail about a quarter of the way along the long edge facing upward and, with a hammer, drive it in about half-way. Do the same thing with another nail half-way along, and a third about three-quarters of the way

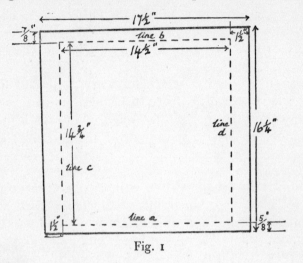

Fig. 1

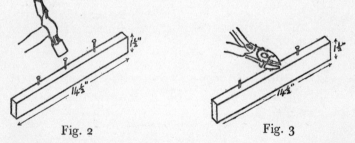

Fig. 2   Fig. 3

along. You don't need to be accurate—judge the distances with your eye. (See Fig. 2.)

Get hold of your pincers or wire-cutters and nip off the heads of those three nails. (See Fig. 3.)

17

Now turn that piece over so that the headless nails are pointing down and place it on the base so that the nails are in line with line ' a ' but not on the line itself—about $\frac{1}{4}''$ inside. (This is so because when the piece is hammered down the outside edge will not protrude over line ' a '.) (See Fig. 4.)

Press down on that piece for a moment and then lift off. You will then see three dents caused by the pressure of the decapitated nails. Place an $1''$ oval nail in the first dent and drive it about half-way in. (See Fig. 5.)

Pull out that nail with a pair of pliers, leaving a small hole. Do the same at the other two dents (using the same nail, if it hasn't bent) and you will have three small holes just inside and along line ' a '.

Pick up the $14\frac{1}{2}''$ by $1\frac{1}{2}''$ piece with the three nails in it and fit it on to the base—by pressing the nails into their corresponding holes, of course. (See Fig. 6.)

(This is the first piece of construction finished. It is the principal upon which all three models are constructed.)

Now take the other $14\frac{1}{2}''$ by $1\frac{1}{2}''$ piece and go through exactly the same process so that it fits against line ' b '. (See Fig. 7.)

When this is done, knock three nails into the long edge of one of the $13\frac{3}{4}''$ by $1\frac{1}{2}''$ pieces, nip off their

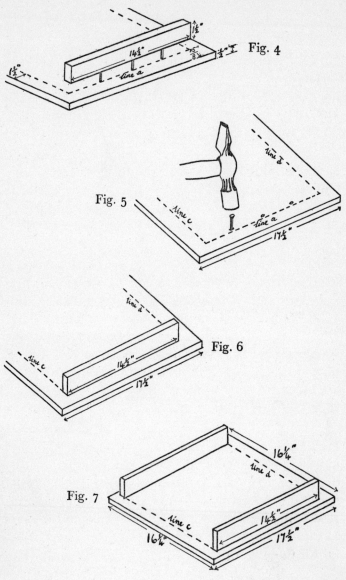

Fig. 4

Fig. 5

Fig. 6

Fig. 7

heads, and place it between the two uprights already in position. Make dents as before etc., and fit that piece in along line ' c '. (See Fig. 8.)

Do the same with the fourth piece to fit it along line ' d '. You now have four upright pieces fitted on the base forming a kind of hollow square.

Into the upper edge of each upright piece drive four or five $\frac{3}{4}''$ veneer-pins about three-quarters to half-way in. Then with your clippers nip off all their heads leaving about a third sticking out. (See Fig. 9.)

From a sheet of plywood saw out a section measuring $14\frac{1}{2}''$ by $14\frac{3}{4}''$. Use a tenon-saw rather than a fret-saw—it's much quicker and gives a straighter edge. Don't forget to smooth it off with sandpaper. This piece will be the floor of the stage itself. Lay it on top of the headless veneer-pins so that its edges are in line with the outside edges of the four uprights. (See Fig. 10.)

Press the plywood down on to the pins—fairly lightly, remove it, turn it over, and you will see the dents running just inside each edge. Into one of the dents tap a veneer-pin so that it just pierces the plywood. Pull it out and go on to make little holes at each dent. (You may find that one pin will not do for making all the holes as it will probably bend

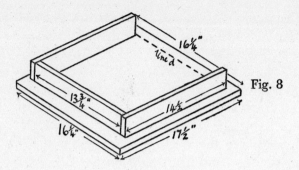

Fig. 8

16¼"

lined

13¾"

14½

16¼"

17½"

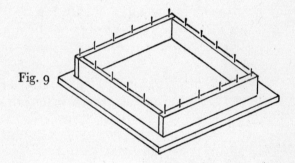

Fig. 9

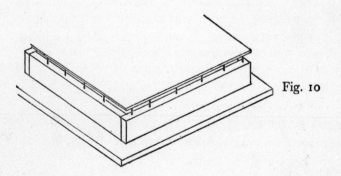

Fig. 10

21

after a few taps). When all the holes are pierced fit the plywood section on to the hollow square. (See Fig. 11.)

From directly above what you have so far constructed will look as in Fig. 12.

The back walls are the next pieces to cut and fit. These, like the base and its upright supports, should be made of ½″ wood to give strength and steadiness to the whole model. You will need three pieces of this wood : one piece measuring 12″ by 6½″ ; and two more, each measuring 10½″ by 4¼″. When you have sawn out these three sections, sandpaper the edges.

Now take the 12″ by 6½″ piece and knock two 1″ oval nails into one of the shorter edges. (See Fig. 13.)

After clipping off the heads of these two nails, turn the section over and press it down on to the plywood floor with the nails in such a position that the outside of the tall wall-piece will fit flush with the back edge of the plywood floor and the two edges 4″ from each side of the floor. (See Fig. 14.)

At the two dents—about ¼″ from the back of the stage—make two holes through the plywood and into the ½″ wood support beneath. Then fit the centre back-wall on to the floor.

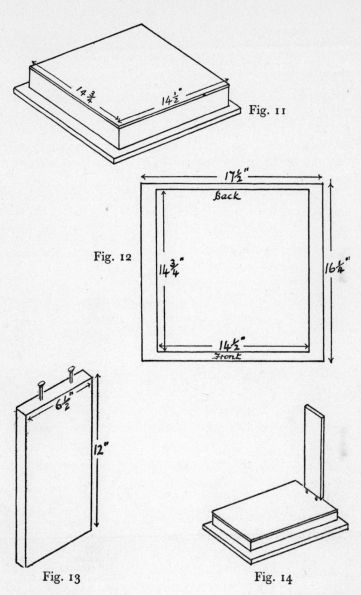

14¾" 14½" Fig. 11

17½"
Back
Fig. 12 14¾" 16¼"
14½"
Front

6½" 12"
Fig. 13

Fig. 14

23

Into the short edge of one of the $10\frac{1}{2}''$ by $4\frac{1}{4}''$ pieces drive two $\frac{3}{4}''$ oval nails—this time as close as possible to the corners. (See Fig. 15.)

Fit this piece on to the stage-floor so that the inner corner of one vertical side touches the inner corner of one of the vertical sides of the centre back-wall section while the opposite corner is $1\frac{7}{8}''$ from the corner of the stage floor. (See Fig. 16.)

When you have done the same thing with the other $10\frac{1}{2}''$ by $4\frac{1}{4}''$ piece on the other side, your back walls are erected. (See Fig. 17.)

Now, having put up these walls, take them down again ! Do this by lifting up the sections with one hand and holding down the plywood floor with the other so that it is not raised. On the inside of the centre back-wall draw a line $3\frac{3}{4}''$ from the bottom and $\frac{3}{4}''$ in from each side, another $6\frac{15}{16}''$ from the bottom, and a third $9\frac{5}{8}''$ from the bottom.

From a length of $\frac{7}{8}''$ lath-wood cut off three pieces each measuring $5''$ long. Drive three veneer-pins into one of the long edges (about half-way in), nip off their heads, press one piece against the inside of the back-centre-wall section so that the top side will fit flush against the lowest line, make holes at the three dents, and push the $5''$ lath piece into position. Do the same with the other two lath-wood pieces—at the centre and the upper lines. (See Fig. 18.)

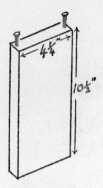

Fig. 15

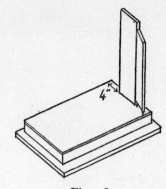

Fig. 16

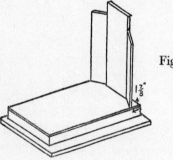

Fig. 17

Fig. 18

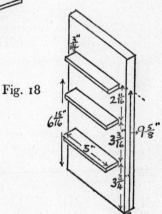

Now cut off six pieces of lath-wood, each 3″ long. On the inside of each of the other back walls (the right and left sections) draw three lines, each $\frac{5}{8}$″ in from the sides, one line $3\frac{3}{4}$″ from the bottom, another $6\frac{15}{16}$″, and a third $10\frac{1}{8}$″ from the bottom. Fix these six pieces into the right and left back-wall sections so that the upper surfaces of them are at the correct heights. (See Fig. 19.)

Replace all three back walls on to the plywood floor.

The next stage in construction is the making and fitting of the other walls and floors of the model—all of plywood. From now on I shall not mention sandpapering each piece after sawing—you can take it for granted. You can also—if you wish and if you have them—use a shooting-board and plane to get 90° edges easily and accurately.

First of all cut two pieces of plywood, each measuring $3\frac{3}{4}$″ by $4\frac{7}{8}$″, and another two, $3\frac{3}{4}$″ by $4\frac{3}{4}$″.

Into one of the long edges of each piece drive two veneer-pins, one about $\frac{1}{4}$″ from one end, and the other about $\frac{1}{2}$″ from the other end. (See Fig. 20.)

You will probably find the driving-in of the pins rather tricky to begin with because the edge of plywood is very narrow (about $\frac{3}{16}$″ thick) and splits fairly easily. If you have been able to afford good-quality plywood the driving-in of the pins will not be difficult, but with cheaper wood you may well have trouble over splitting. To prevent this first

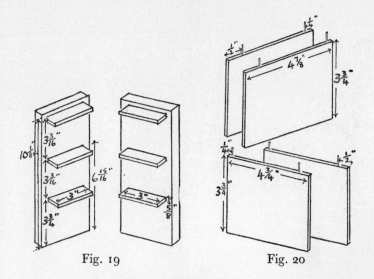

Fig. 19   Fig. 20

tap a pin lightly into the middle of the centre layer
of wood just far enough for it to remain upright.
Then, with your pliers, grip the wood just below
the pin and, with your hammer, knock it in about
half-way—but be careful that it goes in straight or
you will find the point suddenly poking its head out
through one side of the wood. As I said, this will
be tricky to do at first, but you will soon get the
hang of it. (See Fig. 21.)

When you have nipped off the heads of the pins
in the four plywood sections, draw two lines on the
stage floor at right angles to the centre back-wall
$4\frac{3}{8}''$ in from each side of the floor and $4\frac{7}{8}''$ in length
from the inside of the centre back-wall towards
the front of the stage. (See Fig. 22.)

27

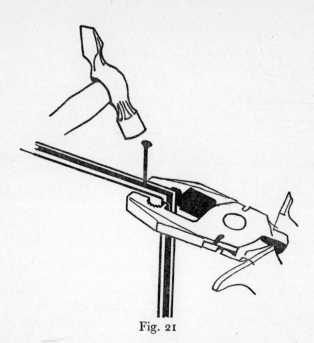

Fig. 21

Take one of the slightly bigger pieces ($3\frac{3}{4}''$ by $4\frac{7}{8}''$) and press it down on the floor so that one side will fit flush with one of the lines you have drawn, and the other side will be nearer the edge of the floor. The edge with the pin about $\frac{1}{4}''$ from the corner should be nearest the centre back-wall. (See Fig. 23.)

Make holes at the dents and fit the piece on. Now do the same with the other larger piece along the other line. Then fit in the smaller ($3\frac{3}{4}''$ by $4\frac{3}{4}''$) pieces so that they stand against the outer sides of the larger pieces with their edges nearer the

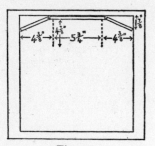

Fig. 22

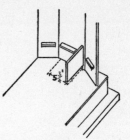

Fig. 23

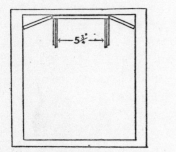

Fig. 24a

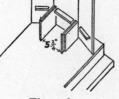

Fig. 24b

$\frac{1}{4}''$ pins tight against the centre back-wall—leaving an $\frac{1}{8}''$ gap between the front edge of the larger pieces and the front edge of the smaller pieces. (See Fig. 24a and Fig. 24b.)

Now cut a piece of plywood $3\frac{3}{4}''$ by $5\frac{3}{4}''$. Knock in a veneer-pin about $\frac{3}{4}''$ from each end and fit this piece on to the stage floor to stand between the inner sides of the $3\frac{3}{4}''$ by $4\frac{7}{8}''$ sections, parallel to the centre back-wall with its side nearer the front of the stage being $2''$ from the inside of the centre back-wall. (See Fig. 25.)

For the last two walls of the ground floor of the model you will need two pieces of plywood, each measuring $3\frac{3}{4}''$ by $4\frac{5}{8}''$. These you should fit on the stage floor so that they stand parallel to the right and left back-walls in a line from the front outer corner of the $3\frac{3}{4}''$ by $4\frac{7}{8}''$ pieces to a point $6\frac{3}{8}''$ from the back corners of the floor itself (the inside edges of these last sections fitting into those $\frac{1}{8}''$ gaps.) (See Fig. 26.)

To complete the ground floor it is necessary to have a number of doorways and doors. If you wish you can paint these on the walls, but it looks better if they are cut out—and, of course, then you can move figures about freely on and off the stage, in and out of the recess etc.

In each of the four walls standing at right angles to the centre back-wall (those measuring $3\frac{3}{4}''$ by $4\frac{7}{8}''$ and $3\frac{3}{4}''$ by $4\frac{3}{4}''$) cut out a rectangle $2\frac{3}{8}''$ high and $1\frac{1}{4}''$ across ; one side of the opening being $\frac{3}{8}''$ from the edge against the centre back-wall, and the other side of the opening being $3\frac{1}{4}''$ or $3\frac{1}{8}''$ (according to the size of the wall) from the edge nearer the front of the stage. (See Fig. 27.)

In the section standing parallel to the centre back-wall ($3\frac{3}{4}''$ by $5\frac{3}{4}''$) cut an opening $2\frac{3}{4}''$ high and $1\frac{3}{4}''$ across, the sides of the opening being $2''$ in from the ends. (See Fig. 28.)

In the middle of each of the remaining two walls ($3\frac{3}{4}''$ by $4\frac{5}{8}''$) cut an opening $3''$ high and $2\frac{1}{8}''$

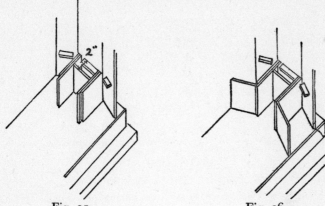

Fig. 25   Fig. 26

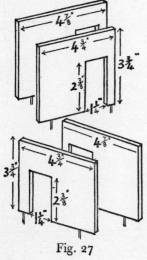

Fig. 27

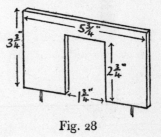

Fig. 28

across—the sides being $1\frac{1}{4}''$ in from the ends. (See Fig. 29.)

To make these openings it is easy enough to saw the vertical cuts with a tenon- or fret-saw, but the transverse cut (across the top of the door) is more difficult. You can use a sharp knife or heavy razor-blade and cut through by drawing the edge of the blade over the plywood again and again (see Fig. 30), or you can use a chisel and hammer, or even an instrument that will pierce a large number of small holes across the top of the doorway so that you can snap the door-piece off.

Replace the four walls at right angles to the back centre-wall (they do not require doors fitted in their openings). The other three walls, however, should be given doors that will push open. To do this, take first of all the $3\frac{3}{4}''$ by $5\frac{3}{4}''$ section and also the little rectangle, $2\frac{3}{4}''$ by $1\frac{3}{4}''$, which you have cut out of it. Round off the two sides and the top of this little piece with sandpaper ; lay the wall down flat with the door piece inside the opening so that the side facing the centre back-wall is uppermost ; cut out a piece of canvas or cloth about $2\frac{1}{2}''$ by $1\frac{1}{2}''$; spread glue on one side of it and stick it down half on the wall and half on the door-piece. (See Fig. 31.)

The other two walls ($3\frac{3}{4}''$ by $4\frac{5}{8}''$) should have double doors in them. These you make exactly the same way as you made and fitted the other door,

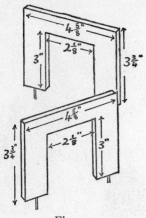

Fig. 29

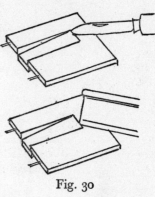

Fig. 30

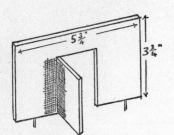

Fig. 31

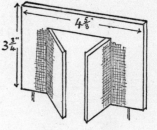

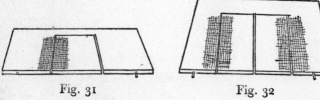

Fig. 32

except that each little rectangle which you had cut out is sawn in half long-ways and then held to its near wall by canvas or cloth. (See Fig. 32.)

When the glue is dry replace the three walls with their doors—and the ground floor is complete. (See Fig. 33.)

From above, the ground floor—its walls and doors indicated by the thick black lines—will now look like the scale-drawing of the Ground-floor Plan, Fig. A.

The next parts to make and fit are the ceilings of the ground floor—or, if you like, the floors of the second storey.

Cut out three pieces of plywood, each measuring $6\frac{1}{8}''$ by $4\frac{3}{4}''$. One of these will be the ceiling over the recess, the others you will use later for two ceilings above that.

Take the $6\frac{1}{8}''$ by $4\frac{3}{4}''$ piece and lay it on the top of the inner walls of the recess. (See Fig. 34.)

Then cut four pieces of the shape and size shown in Fig. 35.

Once you have cut out one of those shapes, the others are easy to measure off. Two of these pieces will be the ceilings on either side of the recess (the other two for ceilings above those later on) and will rest on the tops of the outer walls of the recess, on

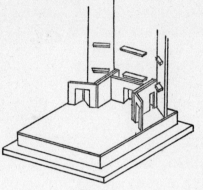

Fig. 33

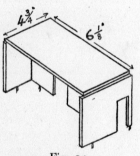

Fig. 34

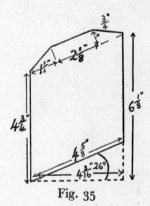

Fig. 35

the 3″ lath pieces low down on the right and left back-walls, and on the walls with double doors. (See Fig. 36.)

The next piece (or wall) to saw should be $6\frac{1}{8}$″ by 3″. In the middle of this cut a doorway (no door is necessary) $2\frac{3}{8}$″ high and $1\frac{1}{4}$″ across, and knock a veneer-pin into the bottom edge about $\frac{1}{2}$″ in from each end. (See Fig. 37.)

Press this section down on to the ceiling of the recess so that it stands directly above the wall with the door ($3\frac{3}{4}$″ by $5\frac{3}{4}$″) across the recess on the ground floor—its front side 2″ from the inside of the centre back-wall. Make holes at the dents right through the plywood ceiling ($6\frac{1}{8}$″ by $4\frac{3}{4}$″) and into the top of the wall beneath. (See Fig. 38.) Then fit in that section.

Now saw two pieces, each measuring 3″ by $4\frac{3}{4}$″, and in each cut an opening $2\frac{3}{8}$″ high and $1\frac{1}{4}$″ across, one side of the opening being $1\frac{1}{4}$″ from one end, and the other side $2\frac{1}{4}$″ from the other end. Knock pins into the bottom edge about $\frac{1}{2}$″ in from each end. (See Fig. 39.)

Press these sections on to the right and left ceilings of the ground floor directly above the outer walls of the recess (see Fig. 40), keeping the doorways nearer the front of the stage.

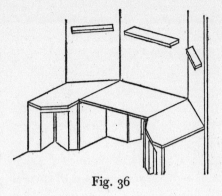

Fig. 36

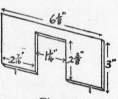
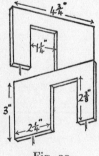

Fig. 37

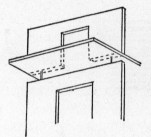

Fig. 38

Fig. 39

Fig. 40

Make holes through the ground-floor ceilings and into the top of the walls beneath, as you did in the last piece of construction—and then fit in those two sections. (See Fig. 41.)

If you now place one of the other $6\frac{1}{8}''$ by $4\frac{3}{4}''$ pieces to rest on the second lath-wood support fixed to the centre back-wall and on the $3''$ by $6\frac{1}{8}''$ first-storey wall, you will have the ceiling of the centre section of the first storey : and if you place the other two pieces of the shape as in Fig. 35 to rest on the second lath-wood supports fixed to the right and left back-walls and on the two second-storey walls with openings ($3''$ by $4\frac{3}{4}''$)—from the front at eye level the model should look as in Fig. 42.

Now for the third storey. Saw a piece of plywood, $2\frac{1}{2}''$ by $6\frac{1}{8}''$, and in the middle of it cut an opening $2''$ high and $1\frac{1}{4}''$ across. Knock a veneer-pin into the bottom edge about $\frac{1}{2}''$ in from each end and—just as you did with the wall in Fig. 38—fix it directly above the wall of the second storey parallel to the centre back-wall. (See Fig. 43.) This will give you three walls fixed into one another up to a height of $9\frac{5}{8}''$ above stage level.

Two more pieces, each measuring $3''$ by $4\frac{1}{2}''$, fit directly above the second-storey walls which in turn fitted directly above the first-storey outer recess walls. These last two walls, however, need not have openings cut into them and, because they

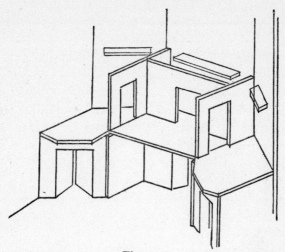

Fig. 41

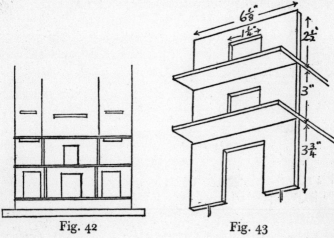

Fig. 42

Fig. 43

39

are slightly shorter—by $\frac{1}{4}''$—than those beneath, there will be a small gap between their front edges and the front edge of the ceiling on which they stand.   (See Fig. 44.)

The last two walls of the third storey, each $3''$ by $4\frac{5}{8}''$, fit on to the second-storey ceilings of the right and left sections, parallel to the right and left back-walls, across the angular projection.   The inner vertical edges will fit into those $\frac{1}{4}''$ gaps by the centre section and the outside vertical edges at the outside corners of the ceilings.   (See Fig. 45.)

For the third-storey ceiling of the centre section use the last of the $6\frac{1}{8}''$ by $4\frac{3}{4}''$ pieces and place it resting on the third lath-wood support of the centre back-wall and on the third storey wall parallel to the centre back-wall.   (See Fig. 46.)

For the third-storey ceilings of the right and left sections you will need two pieces shaped as in Fig. 35, but without the angular projection—that is a parallelogram $4\frac{5}{8}''$ by $4\frac{3}{4}''$ at an angle of $26°$. Place these as in Fig. 47.

The last wall of the model measures $2\frac{3}{8}''$ by $6\frac{1}{8}''$ and this stands along the front edge of the third-storey ceiling—fixed in with pins.   (See Fig. 48.)

Now for the roof sections. To cover the centre section of the model you need two rectangular

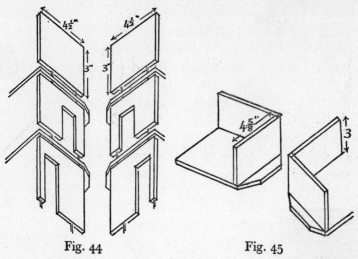

Fig. 44

Fig. 45

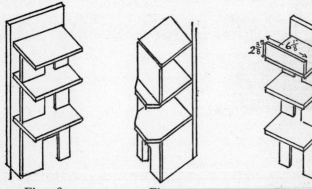

Fig. 46   Fig. 47   Fig. 48

pieces, one measuring $6\frac{1}{4}''$ by $3\frac{1}{4}''$, and the other $6\frac{1}{4}''$ by $3\frac{1}{8}''$. Just in from one of the long edges of the larger piece drive three veneer-pins at equal distances from one another so that the points just break through the wood. Then place one of the long edges of the smaller piece at right angles to the larger so that the pin points stick into the edge of the former. (See Fig. 49.)

Now hammer the pins right in and then bend the two pieces out at an obtuse angle of about 125°. (See Fig. 50.)

This will now fit over the centre section, one long edge resting on the top of the centre back-wall, and the other just over the top edge of the vertical $6\frac{1}{8}''$ by $2\frac{3}{8}''$ fourth-storey wall. (See Fig. 51.)

For the roofs over the right and left sections of the model saw four parallelograms, two measuring $4\frac{3}{4}''$ by $3\frac{1}{4}''$ and two measuring $4\frac{3}{4}''$ by $3\frac{1}{8}''$. (See Fig. 52.)

These fit exactly the same way as the centre section roof. (See Fig. 53.)

The model is now constructed except for a number of additional smaller parts.

Between the first- and second-storey ceilings of the right and left sections at the front you will need

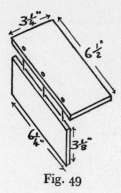

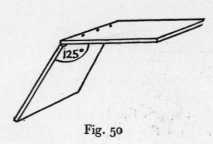

Fig. 49

Fig. 50

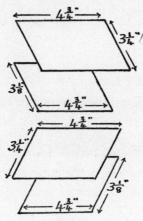

Fig. 52

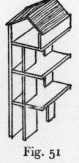

Fig. 51

Fig. 53

window-walls to form two bow windows which project over the walls below. Six sections are necessary : four measuring $3\frac{3}{8}''$ by $1\frac{5}{8}''$ and two measuring $3\frac{3}{8}''$ by $2\frac{1}{8}''$. To fix these in position drive two veneer-pins into each face of the projecting ceilings and nip off their heads to leave about $\frac{1}{8}''$ sticking out. (See Fig. 54.)

Now press the two larger sections ($3\frac{3}{8}''$ by $2\frac{1}{8}''$) up against these pins in the centre faces, and the four smaller sections ($3\frac{3}{8}''$ by $1\frac{5}{8}''$) against the other faces. Drive holes through at the dents and then fit them into position. (See Fig. 55.)

You will find that they do not fit tightly against one another, and to remedy this you will have to sandpaper off the vertical edges at angles—the little black triangles in Fig. 56.

Now comes a difficult bit : the making of windows in the two central front-walls of the projecting bows and also in the front wall of the fourth storey of the centre section. You can of course just paint them in later, but, if you can spare the time, openings which are cut out look much better. As in the making of the doorways it will be necessary to use a knife, razor blade, chisel or some sort of spike— but all four sides of each opening (not just one) will have to be cut out carefully. It is up to you what shape these windows take, although I have given one possible plan in Fig. 57.

44

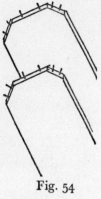

Fig. 54

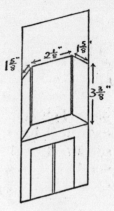

Fig. 55

Fig. 56

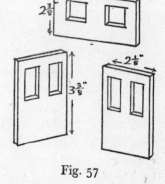

Fig. 57

There is, as you see, no front wall in the second-storey centre section of the model—nor in the storey above that. These two rooms are the lower and upper galleries. (The lower used as an additional acting area, and the upper as a gallery for musicians or even yet another acting area.) Each of them will need a rail or balustrade. For the lower one cut a piece of plywood 6″ by $\frac{3}{8}$″ and along the middle make five small holes. Now take five ordinary match-sticks and cut both ends of each to a point so that you have five miniature stakes. Fit these into the plywood as in Fig. 58. Then place the balustrade, match-stick points down, on the ceiling of the first storey just a little way in from the front edge. Where the ends of the match-sticks rest on the ceiling make five small holes—and you can fit in the balustrade. You can see it—and the one above—in position in Fig. 61. For the rail at the front of the upper gallery cut another piece of ply-wood also 6″ by $\frac{3}{8}$″. This time, however, make seven little holes along the middle and, using smaller match-sticks (such as Swan Vestas) fit them in. (See Fig. 59.)

Below each bow-window two curved supporting brackets make the construction look better. For these cut out four little pieces $1\frac{15}{16}$″ by $1\frac{1}{8}$″ and, as in Fig. 60, make a curve using a knife or fret-saw. Knock two veneer-pins into each of the $1\frac{1}{8}$″ edges, clip their heads and press them up against the two front walls of the ground floor (the ones with double doors) so that you have a bracket with its top side against the under side of the first-storey ceiling on each side of the double doors. You will see this best in the Isometric Projection Drawing F (page 61).

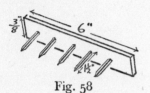

Fig. 58

Fig. 59

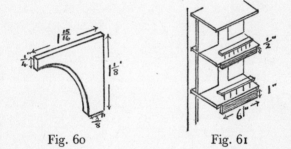

Fig. 60

Fig. 61

For the final piece of construction of the building itself two pelmets to conceal the tops of curtains which can be drawn across the front of the recess and the lower gallery are needed. Make these from two narrow pieces of plywood, one measuring 6″ by 1″ and the other 6″ by ½″. With pins fix them on to the front edges of the first- and second-storey ceilings of the centre section. (See Fig. 61.)

47

If you read the chapter on the development of the theatre you may remember that there was a roof sheltering most of the stage in the open-air Elizabethan playhouse. This is the final thing to make.

From a length of $\frac{3}{4}''$ dowel-rod, cut two pieces $6\frac{1}{2}''$ long. In one end of each drive a veneer-pin about half-way at the centre, and in the other end of each, two pins near the circumference. (See Fig. 62.)

The bases for these two columns you can make from two blocks of wood, $1''$ by $1''$ by $1\frac{1}{2}''$ (see Fig. 63), round the tops and bottoms of which you can fix strips of plywood. (Another way, however, is to take two blocks $1\frac{1}{2}''$ by $1\frac{1}{2}''$ by $1\frac{1}{2}''$ and cut out four sunken faces in each.)

If you choose the first method you will need four little strips of plywood measuring $\frac{3}{8}''$ by $1\frac{5}{16}''$, and another four measuring $\frac{3}{8}''$ by $1''$. At the bottom of the two blocks fix the larger strips opposite each other, and the smaller strips in between. (See Fig. 64.)

Round the top of the two blocks fix—in the same way—four strips measuring $\frac{1}{4}''$ by $1\frac{5}{16}''$, and four measuring $\frac{1}{4}''$ by $1''$. (See Fig. 65.)

In the centre of the top of each block make a hole with a veneer-pin and fit on the columns. (See Fig. 66.)

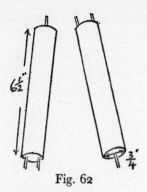

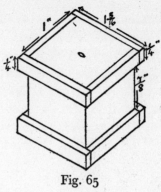

Fig. 62

Fig. 65

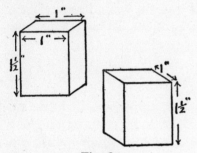

Fig. 63

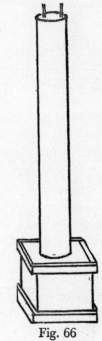

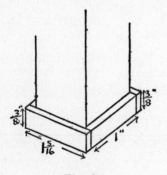

Fig. 64

Fig. 66

To complete the columns you want capitals. These can be made also from blocks of wood which can be carved to any shape you like and fitted on the two pins. One method, which is illustrated, is to use two cotton reels. Leave the top end of each reel as it is, but cut down the drum and the bottom beading so that the shaft tapers down to a circle $\frac{13}{16}''$ in diameter. (See Fig. 67.)

Now you can paint on decoration for these capitals —or, better still, make a solid moulding. If you wish to do the latter to produce a Corinthian type of capital, cut out a piece of thin tin to the shape in Fig. 68.

This can be done with scissors provided the tin is thin enough. (It is possible to get a small sheet of thin brass from some craft-shops—and this makes it even easier.)

From your little piece of metal cut out a leaf-crown shape as in Fig. 69 and bend out and over the tops of each leaf-shape. Be careful when you do this or you will cut the tips of your fingers—especially if you are using tin. Then bend the crown round the lower half of the cotton-reel drum and knock in a couple of tacks or pins through the tin and into the wood at the back to hold it firmly. Now make two holes at the bottom of each capital near the edge for the pins on the top of each column. (See Fig. 70.)

Fig. 67

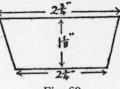

Fig. 68

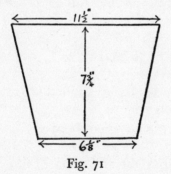

Fig. 69

Fig. 70

Fig. 71

Fit the capitals on to the columns. For the roof over the stage saw a piece of plywood, $7\frac{3}{4}''$ wide, $11\frac{1}{2}''$ along one length and $6\frac{1}{8}''$ along the other. (See Fig. 71.)

Into the shorter edge drive three veneer-pins, nip off their heads, and press it against the front edge of the third-storey ceiling. (See Fig. 72.) Make holes at the dents, but don't fit in the roof until the columns are set up on the stage floor to support it.

Now, on the stage floor draw two squares, $1\frac{5}{16}''$ along the sides, $2''$ from the front of the stage and $2''$ in from the sides. Turn your column bases over and into the bottom drive three veneer-pins to form a triangle. (See Fig. 73.)

Press these on to the squares drawn on the stage floor, make holes at the dents, fit the shafts and capitals back on, push the whole columns on to the stage, press the roof into the third-storey ceiling and allow it to rest on the top of the capitals. (See Fig. 74.)

The last pieces to make are little roof-sections for the bow-windows. Cut two pieces of plywood, $2\frac{1}{8}''$ by $1\frac{1}{4}''$, and four triangles $1\frac{5}{8}''$ along the bases and $1\frac{1}{4}''$ along the shorter sides. (See Fig. 75.) If you sandpaper the edges at a fairly acute angle these will then fit neatly over the bow-windows, the bottoms resting on the tops of the faces of the projections, and the tops against the walls above. (See Fig. 76.)

The model theatre is now complete in construction. All that remains to do now is to paint the model.

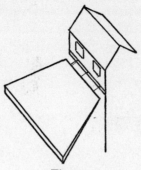

Fig. 72

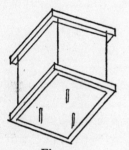

Fig. 73

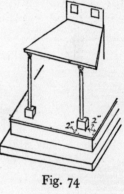

Fig. 74

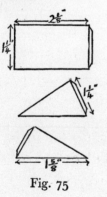

Fig. 75

Fig. 76

53

The colour is up to you. One suggestion, which you may follow if you wish, is to leave the stage floor, the inside walls and ceilings as they are—a natural wood ; the walls and doors facing the front you can paint white or pale grey, and the roofs red or reddish-brown.

Perhaps the best kind of paint to use is emulsion as it dries quickly with a good dull surface. Matt oil paint is perfectly satisfactory, though it dries more slowly. Poster paint, however, is not so good : the plywood will soak it up, so that it is useless unless the wood is first painted over with some other medium.

The wooden joists and jambs of an Elizabethan building were generally visible on the outside. These you can indicate by pasting on strips of cardboard up the sides of the walls and doorways and windows, which are best in a dark colour— brown or black or dark grey. You can see a possible arrangement of these in the photograph of the completed model in the frontispiece.

As I mentioned before, the recess on the ground floor and the gallery above can be curtained off. If you fix a short length of wire behind the pelmet of each, you can then run a piece of cloth (any colour you like) from the wire to pull across the openings.

This model theatre is, of course, just the right kind of stage to use for Shakespeare's plays. The gallery gives you a balcony for such scenes as Juliet's room ; the recess can be used to set up a

54

throne, to provide a hiding place for Polonius, or a cave for Caliban ; the bow-windows can act as part of a street of houses ; and the large double doors are the main means of entrances and exits—particularly for opposing armies.

It is possible to buy cut-out figures of characters in plays which you can place wherever you wish or push on and off with wires—but you can make them yourself or find them in books. Scenery, of course, is not very important for this theatre—an odd tree, bench, table or chair is often sufficient.

To help you in your building there are these scale drawings of the theatre.

Fig. A   Ground-floor Plan

Fig. B   Second-storey Plan

Fig. C   Roof Plan

Fig. D   Front Elevation

Fig. E   Cross Section

and also in proportion, but not to scale

Fig. F   Isometric Projection

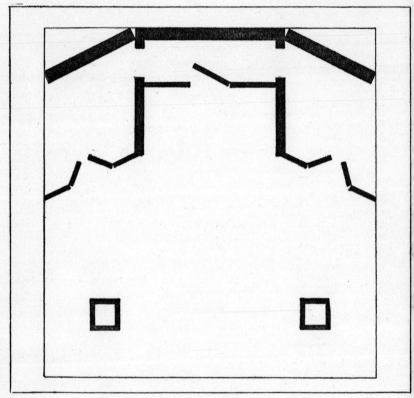

Fig. A   Ground-floor Plan.   Scale 1 : 4

Eighteenth-century theatre

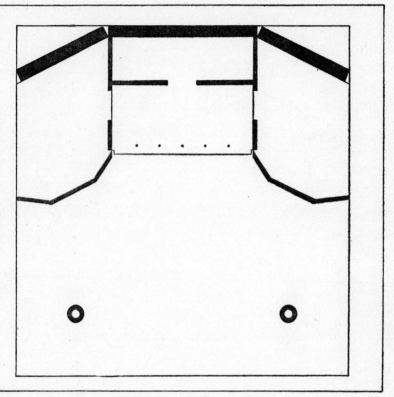

Fig. B   Second-storey Plan.   Scale 1 : 4

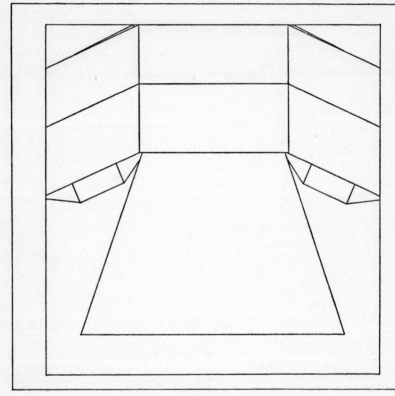

Fig. C   Roof Plan.   Scale 1 : 4

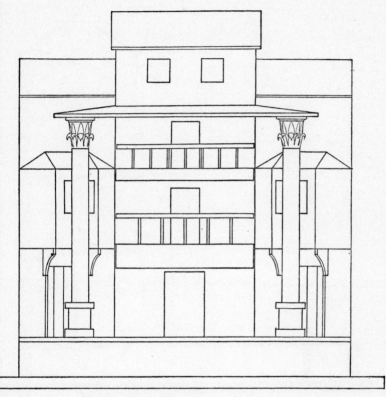

Fig. D   Front Elevation.   Scale 1 : 4

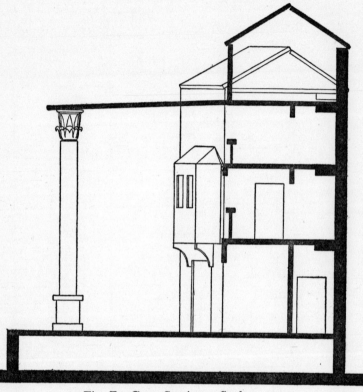

Fig. E   Cross Section.   Scale 1 : 4

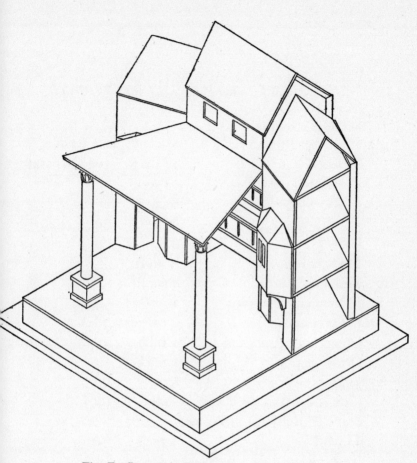

Fig. F   Isometric Projection.   Not to scale

Materials required :

		from
Plywood	11 sq. ft.	7s 9d to 9s 9d
1″ Hard-wood	2¼ sq. ft.	
½″ Hard-wood	6 sq. ft.	
⅞″ Lath-wood	8 ft.	8d to 1s 4d
Wire	6 ft.	2d
Thick cardboard	5 sq. ft.	
Thin cardboard	2 sq. ft.	
¾″ Veneer/Panel pins	1 packet	6d
1″ Oval nails	4 oz.	7d
Glue	1 tube	1s 3d
Drawing-pins	1 packet	
½″ Staples	4 oz.	9d
(Screw-eyes)	(25)	(9d)
Paint (Emulsion/Oil/Poster)		
Thread	2 reels	

Total   from 10s 8d to 14s 4d

Tools required :

Hammer, saw (for hard-wood), tenon-saw (for plywood and lath-wood), wire-cutters, pliers, ruler (with $\frac{1}{8}$s and $\frac{1}{16}$s), pencil, compasses, set-square or triangle, sandpaper, knife or razor blade, paint brushes. (Additional tools—not essential: plane, fret-saw, shooting-board, hack-saw, spirit-level.)

The base of the model of the Eighteenth-century Theatre is best made of 1″ wood, and the back and side walls of ½″ wood. For these you should be able to get sufficient material from old boxes or crates.

The back wall can be cut from a piece measuring 1′ 7¾″ by 1′ 7⅝″ and angled down on one of the 1′ 7¾″ sides to 1′ 1⅝″. (See Fig. 1.)

After sawing any section don't forget to sandpaper the edges—even the smallest plywood pieces.

The base—of 1″ wood—should measure 1′ 6¾″ by 1′ 3″. Into one of the longer edges drive three ¾″ oval nails about half-way in, and then nip off the heads of these nails—see Figs 2 and 3 of the Elizabethan Theatre Instructions. (See Fig. 2.)

Now take the back-wall piece and press this against the oval nails so that the back wall projects ½″ from each side of the base. (See Fig. 3.)

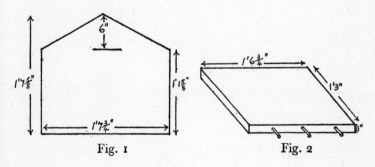

Fig. 1   Fig. 2

At the points where the nails have made dents in the back wall drive three holes with a $\frac{3}{4}''$ oval nail (one will do provided it doesn't get bent). You can then fit the base on to the back wall, each decapitated nail going into its corresponding hole in the back wall. (See Fig. 4.)

Into each of the shorter edges of the base drive three $\frac{3}{4}''$ oval nails and nip off their heads. (See Fig. 5.)

It is now time to saw the two side walls, each measuring $1'\ 1\frac{5}{8}''$ by $1'\ 3''$ (of $\frac{1}{2}''$ wood). Place one of these against one of the sides of the base with its three nails sticking out, and press fairly hard so that three dents are left. At the dents make three holes and then fit the base on to that side wall. (See Fig. 6.)

Do the same with the other side wall and the outer walls and base of the model are completed. (See Fig. 7.)

Next saw two pieces of $\frac{1}{2}''$ wood, measuring $6\frac{1}{8}''$ by $2''$; two pieces, $6\frac{1}{8}''$ by $3\frac{3}{8}''$; and one piece, $11\frac{1}{2}''$ by $2''$. (See Fig. 8.)

Into one of the longer edges of each piece drive two oval nails about half-way in and nip off their heads. Take one of the $6\frac{1}{8}''$ by $2''$ sections and

64

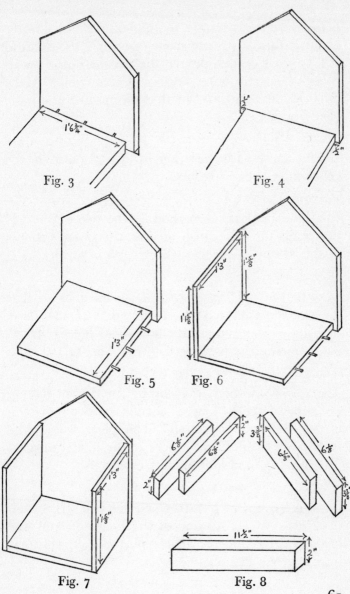

Fig. 3

Fig. 4

Fig. 5

Fig. 6

Fig. 7

Fig. 8

press it on to the base so that one of the shorter edges is flush with the front edge of the base, and the vertical corner nearer the nearer outside wall is $4\frac{1}{8}''$ from the outer corner of that wall. Make holes at the dents and fit that piece on to the base. (See Fig. 9.)

Do the same with the other $6\frac{1}{8}''$ by $2''$ piece on the other side. (See Fig. 10.)

Employing the same method fix the two $6\frac{1}{8}''$ by $3\frac{3}{8}''$ pieces on the base flush against the outer surfaces of the $6\frac{1}{8}''$ by $2''$ pieces. (See Figs 11a and 11b.)

Now fit the $11\frac{1}{2}''$ by $2''$ section on the base so that it stands parallel to the front edge of the base, with its two ends against the ends of the $6\frac{1}{8}''$ by $2''$ pieces facing the back wall. (See Fig. 12.)

A piece of plywood, $11\frac{1}{2}''$ by $6\frac{5}{8}''$, will then rest on the tops of the $6\frac{1}{8}''$ by $2''$ sections and on the top of the $11\frac{1}{2}''$ by $6\frac{5}{8}''$ section. This piece will be the small area of auditorium floor of the model theatre. (See Fig. 13, and also Scale Drawing A.)

From a length of $\frac{7}{8}''$ lath-wood cut two strips each measuring $8''$. Into one of the long edges of one of them drive three $\frac{3}{4}''$ veneer pins and nip off their heads. (See Fig. 14.)

66

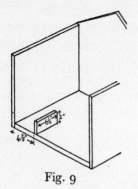

Fig. 9

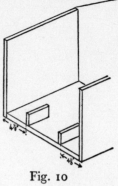

Fig. 10

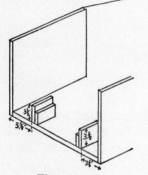

Fig. 11a

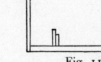

Fig. 11b

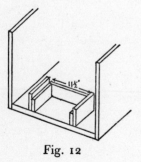

Fig. 12

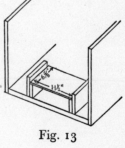

Fig. 13

67

Press these headless pins against the inside of one of the side walls so that the upper surface of the lath-wood piece is $1\frac{5}{8}''$ above the upper surface of the base, one end being $\frac{1}{2}''$ from the inside of the back wall and the other $6\frac{1}{2}''$ from the front edge of the side wall. Make holes at the dents with a veneer-pin and fit the lath-wood piece on to the side wall. (See Figs. 15a and 15b.)

Do the same with the other $8''$ lath-wood sections on the other side wall. (See Fig. 16.)

Now cut a piece of plywood measuring $1'\,6\frac{3}{8}''$ by $6\frac{1}{2}''$. This will rest upon the two lath-wood strips spanning the base of the model with one long edge about $1''$ from the inside of the back wall. (See Fig. 17.)

(This plywood section will be used later on as a base for the flats which slide through grooves in the floor of the stage itself. See also Scale Drawing B.)

The next job is the making and fitting of the stage floor. In the eighteenth-century theatre this floor sloped—sometimes fairly steeply—from the back wall to the front edge of the stage. This slope helped to give the effect of distance from front to back of the stage and was (and is still) called the 'rake'. Because the floor sloped it means that the supports for the floor must slope as well, higher at the back than at the front.

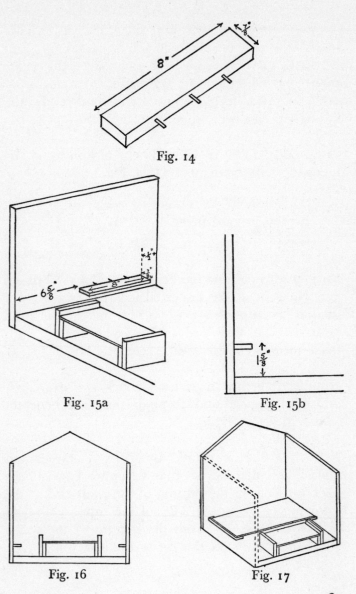

Fig. 14

Fig. 15a

Fig. 15b

Fig. 16

Fig. 17

69

To fit these supports (and also supports at higher levels—the purpose of which will be explained later) you will have to remove the two side walls of the model. Having done so, lay one of them down flat with the inside facing upward and remove also the lath-wood support. (See Fig. 18.)

From odd lengths of $\frac{1}{2}''$ wood cut ten pieces of the following measurements : (See Fig. 19.)

six pieces measuring $1'\ 3''$ by $\frac{3}{4}''$ by $\frac{1}{2}''$

two pieces measuring $8\frac{7}{8}''$ by $\frac{3}{4}''$ by $\frac{1}{2}''$

two pieces measuring $6\frac{1}{8}''$ by $\frac{3}{4}''$ by $\frac{1}{2}''$

First of all take one of the $6\frac{1}{8}''$ by $\frac{3}{4}''$ by $\frac{1}{2}''$ pieces and place it on the upper surface of the side wall so that its upper edge—$\frac{1}{2}''$ wide—is $4\frac{3}{8}''$ from the bottom of the wall and its front edge is flush with the front edge of the wall. (See Fig. 20.)

Holding it firmly in position knock two oval nails into the support and through the wall beneath. (See Figs. 21 and 22.)

Now take one of the $8\frac{7}{8}''$ by $\frac{3}{4}''$ by $\frac{1}{2}''$ pieces and place it on the wall so that its upper edge at the back is $4\frac{3}{4}''$ from the bottom of the wall, and at the front meets the upper edge of the support already in position (i.e. $4\frac{3}{8}''$ from the bottom of the wall). With three nails fix this on to the side wall. (See Fig. 23.)

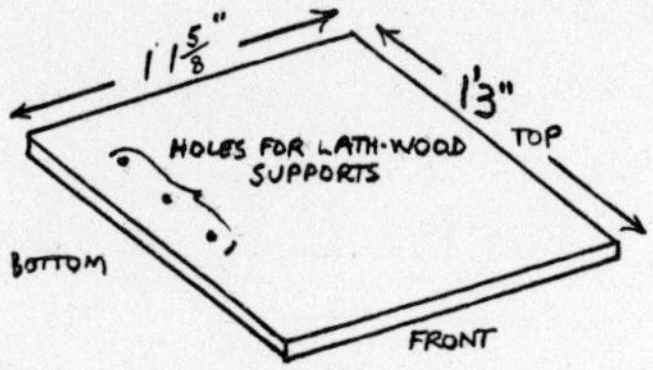
1' 1 5/8"
1'3"
HOLES FOR LATH-WOOD SUPPORTS
TOP
BOTTOM
FRONT
Fig. 18

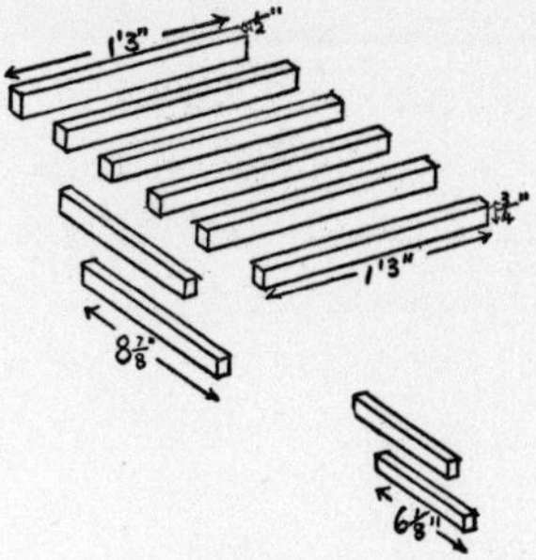
1'3"
1'3"
8 7/8"
6 1/8"
Fig. 19

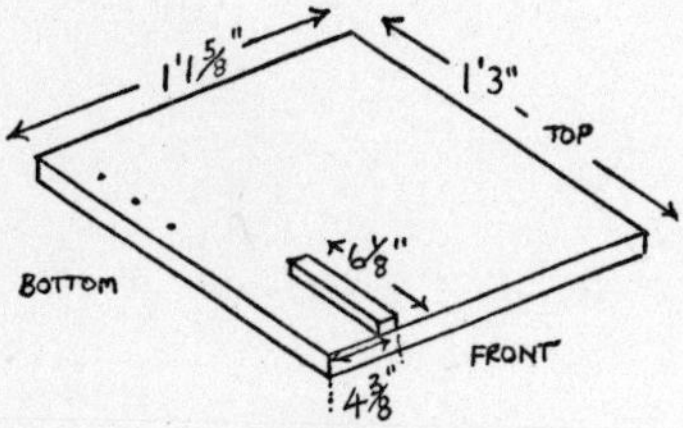
1' 1 5/8"
1'3"
TOP
BOTTOM
6 1/8"
FRONT
4 3/8"
Fig. 20

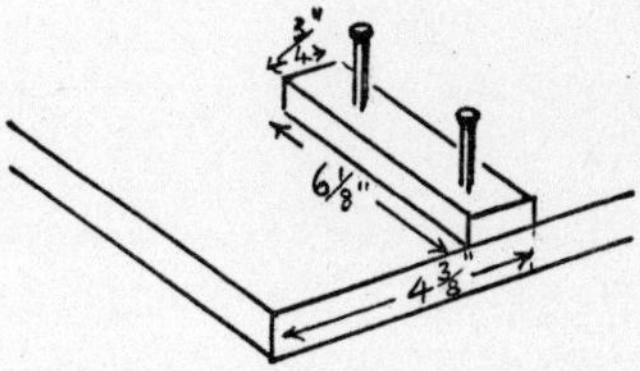
6 1/8"
4 3/8"
Fig. 21

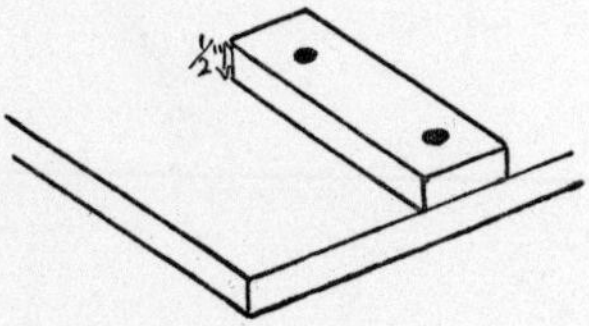
Fig. 22

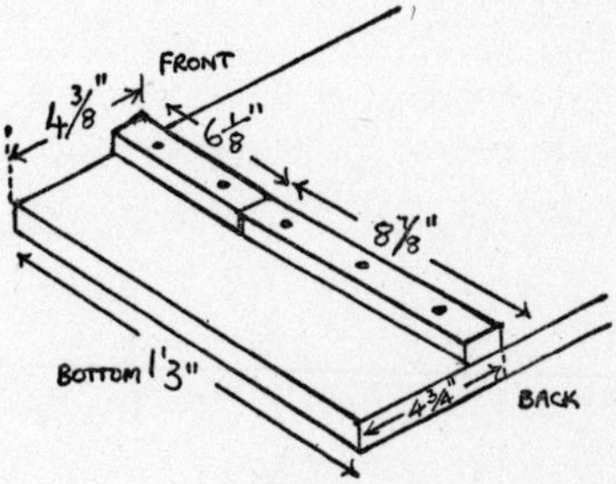
FRONT
4 3/8"
6 1/8"
8 7/8"
BOTTOM 1'3"
4 3/4"
BACK
Fig. 23

Place three of the 1′ 3″ by ¾″ by ½″ on the same inside wall so that the upper edge of the first is 7¾″ from the bottom of the wall, of the second 10¾″, and of the third 1′ 1⅝″. These three pieces, however, are parallel to the top and bottom of the side wall —they do not slope at an angle. Fix each of them in position with four or five oval nails. (See Fig. 24.)

When you have done the same with the other supports on the other side wall, replace the lath-wood sections, fit the side walls back on to the base and put back the 1′ 6⅜″ by 6½″ plywood section. From directly in front the model will now appear as in Fig. 25.

It is now time to make the stage floor itself. For this you will need a piece of plywood measuring 1′ 6⅜″ by 1′ 1¼″. It is better—for this particular section—to use good-quality plywood, preferably with a mahogany finish. (See Fig. 26.)

On one of the surfaces of the plywood draw a line across, parallel with the 1′ 6⅜″ edges, 4⅝″ in from one edge ; and another 2¾″ in from the same edge. And, parallel with the 1′ 1¼″ edges, draw two lines 3⁷⁄₁₆″ in from those edges. (See Fig. 27.)

With a pair of compasses draw an arc from the centre point of the front edge of the plywood to meet the intersection of the lines 3⁷⁄₁₆″ from the sides and the line 2¾″ from the front. The shaded

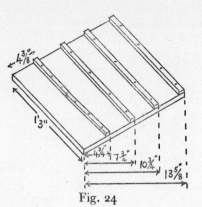

Fig. 24

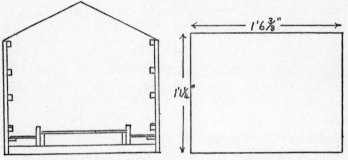

Fig. 25

Fig. 26

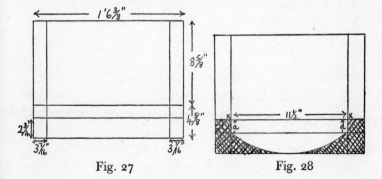

Fig. 27

Fig. 28

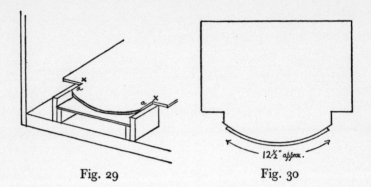

Fig. 29   Fig. 30

area on the diagram can then be cut away—
preferably with a fret-saw.   (See Fig. 28.)

This then is your stage floor and can be placed
resting on the sloping supports fixed on the side
walls (the 8⅞″ long pieces) with its front edge 1¾″
from the front of the base.   The two corners
marked ' x ' in Fig. 28 should be just above the
two inside back corners of the high supports fixed
on the base (6⅛″ by 3⅜″ in Figs. 11a and 11b) and
the two short sides marked ' a ' in Fig. 28 flush
with the inside vertical surfaces of the same pieces.
(See Fig. 29.)

The next piece—the curved vertical front edge of
the stage floor—is rather tricky.   For it you will
need a strip of plywood 1¼″ by 1′ ½″ approximately.
(I say ' approximately ' because the measurement
round the curved edge of the stage is best done by
yourself, using a length of string or thread, leaving

74

about $\frac{3}{16}''$ in from each end of the curve. (See Fig. 30.)

This strip of plywood is easier to work with and less likely to crack if it is fairly thick—about $\frac{1}{5}''$ thick if possible. Lay it down flat and, using a small, thin-bladed saw, make about forty-one to fifty-one cuts (an odd number is essential—for some strange reason !) through the two top layers of wood. (See Fig. 31.)

Then bend this strip over the curve—the top being flush with the upper surface of the stage floor—and knock about nine or ten $\frac{1}{2}''$ veneer-pins through the strip and into the front edge of the curve. (See Fig. 32.) (It may help you, incidentally, if you also use strong glue to fix the strip on to the curved edge first.) This particular operation is complicated, but it may prevent you from losing your temper—

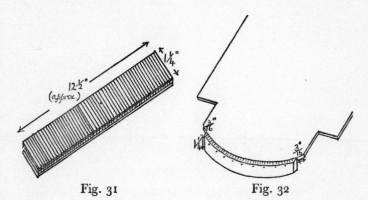

Fig. 31   Fig. 32

because if you try to do it in a simpler way the strip is almost certain to snap.

Now you can replace the stage floor and the bottom of the strip will rest on the small area of auditorium floor.

The next pieces to make are the floors for the lower stage boxes and galleries. For these cut two pieces of plywood each measuring $6\frac{1}{8}''$ by $3\frac{5}{8}''$. They will rest on the tops of the higher supports on the base and on the $6\frac{1}{8}''$ supports fixed to the side walls. To fix them firmly knock two veneer-pins into the tops of each base support, nip off their heads, press the plywood pieces down, remove, make holes at the dents and fit the floors in. (See Figs. 33a and 33b.)

From the front the model should now look as in Fig. 34.

It is now time to build the inner walls—all of plywood. First cut out two pieces, each measuring $9\frac{1}{16}''$ by $4\frac{1}{4}''$. These will stand along the back edges of the lower boxes and on the stage floor itself. But, of course, they won't fit in because of the supports running along the side walls—cuts will have to be made in the supports to take their outer vertical edges. Remove, therefore, the side walls and lay them flat with the supports uppermost. Then, with

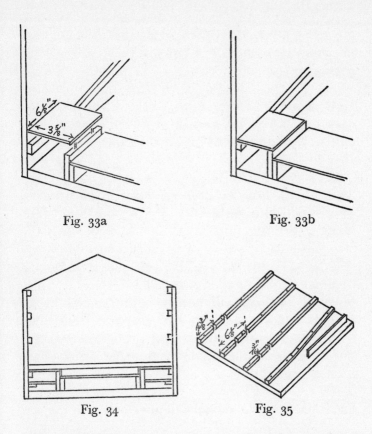

Fig. 33a   Fig. 33b

Fig. 34   Fig. 35

a thin-bladed saw, cut out from each of the top three supports a small section $\frac{3}{16}''$ wide—the edge of each cut nearer the back wall being $6\frac{1}{8}''$ from the front edge of the wall. Cut through the supports but not into the walls themselves. (See Fig. 35.)

Having done this to the supports on each side wall, cut out six other little sections $\frac{3}{16}''$ wide from the top three supports on each wall—this time the back of each cut being $4\frac{3}{8}''$ from the front of the wall. (See Fig. 36.)

Now replace the side walls. One vertical edge of each $9\frac{1}{16}''$ by $4\frac{1}{8}''$ piece will fit into the set of three cuts in the supports $6\frac{1}{8}''$ from the front of the walls. (See Fig. 37.)

Two more plywood pieces, each measuring $9''$ by $3\frac{5}{8}''$, will fit into the cuts $4\frac{1}{8}''$ from the front of the walls. (See Fig. 38.)

Another two pieces, $9\frac{1}{16}''$ by $4\frac{1}{4}''$ will stand on the floors of the side galleries parallel to the side walls, but each of them will need two veneer-pins in the bottom edge to go into two corresponding holes in the floor to hold them firm. These two pieces stand $1\frac{1}{4}''$ from the inside of the side walls. (See Figs. 39 and 40.)

From the front the model will now look as in Fig. 41.

Next cut two pieces of plywood, $9\frac{1}{16}''$ by $2\frac{3}{4}''$. These will stand on the stage floor at an angle from the inside vertical corners of the $9''$ by $4\frac{1}{8}''$ pieces to points $7\frac{7}{8}''$ from the front of the base. Into the bottom edge of each piece drive two veneer-pins $\frac{1}{4}''$ in from each end. Press these pieces on to the stage floor in their correct positions, make holes at the dents and then fit them in. (See Fig. 42.)

78

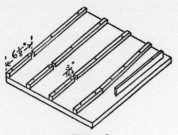

Fig. 36

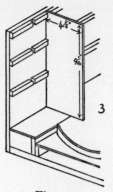

3

Fig. 37

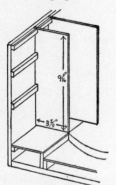

Fig. 38

Fig. 39

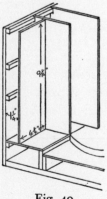

Fig. 40

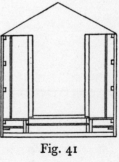

Fig. 41

When doing this you will find out that the outer vertical edges do not fit tightly against the inner vertical edges of the 9″ by 4⅛″ pieces, and that, because of the slight slope of the stage floor from front to back they will lean forward. To get a tight fit and a properly vertical position you will have to sandpaper off at an angle the edges marked ‘ a ’ and ‘ b ’ in Fig. 42.

Although all the main inner and outer walls of the model are now constructed you have not yet finished with them because a number of doors have to be cut in them and supports fixed on them to take the upper floors of the boxes and galleries. These will come later, however.

The next pieces to make are the arches which span the openings over the stage between the $9\frac{1}{16}$″ by $4\frac{1}{8}$″ and $9\frac{1}{16}$″ by $2\frac{3}{4}$″ walls. For these cut two pieces of plywood, one measuring $10\frac{1}{8}$″ by 3″, the other $6\frac{3}{8}$″ by 3″. (See Fig. 43.)

On the larger piece draw a line parallel to the 3″ sides 1″ in from each end, and mark a point on each of those lines $1\frac{1}{4}$″ from one of the long sides. Then mark another point half-way along and $\frac{7}{16}$″ in from the other long side. (See Fig. 44.)

Call these points ‘ a ’, ‘ b ’ and ‘ c ’. With your compasses draw an arc running from ‘ a ’ to ‘ c ’ to ‘ b ’, and two smaller arcs from each bottom

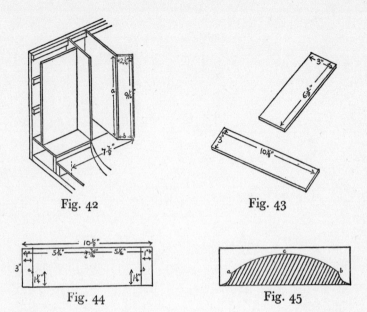

Fig. 42

Fig. 43

Fig. 44

Fig. 45

corner to ' a ' and ' b '—these two curving the
other way from the first. With a fret-saw saw out
the shaded area in Fig. 45.

Now take the other piece, $6\frac{3}{8}''$ by $3''$. On it draw
a line $1''$ in from and parallel to each $3''$ edge,
and mark two points ' x ' and ' y ' on them half-
way along ; then mark a third point ' z ' half-way
along and $1\frac{1}{8}''$ in from one of the longer edges. (See
Fig. 46.)

Draw a curve from ' x ' to ' z ' to ' y ', and another
two from the bottom corners to ' x ' and ' y '. Cut
out the shaded area as in Fig. 47.

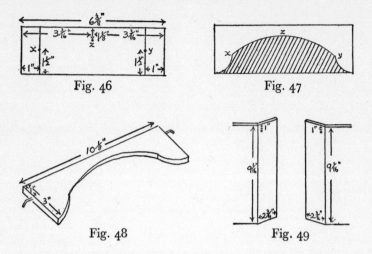

Fig. 46

Fig. 47

Fig. 48

Fig. 49

The larger curved piece will span the stage opening from the top and front of the two $9\frac{1}{16}''$ by $2\frac{3}{4}''$ sections. To fit this on, sandpaper each $3''$ edge at an angle ; knock in a veneer-pin into each $3''$ edge and bend it back slightly. (See Fig. 48.)

Nip off the heads of these pins and then press the $3''$ ends against the $9\frac{1}{16}''$ and $2\frac{3}{4}''$ pieces so that the pins make dents $1\frac{1}{2}''$ down from the top of each piece and almost at the vertical edge which joins the $9\frac{1}{16}''$ by $4\frac{1}{8}''$ section. (See Fig. 49.)

Now fit the arch across. (See Fig. 50.)

Do the same with the smaller arch so that it fits into the $9\frac{1}{16}''$ by $2\frac{3}{4}''$ pieces farther back. (See Fig. 51.)

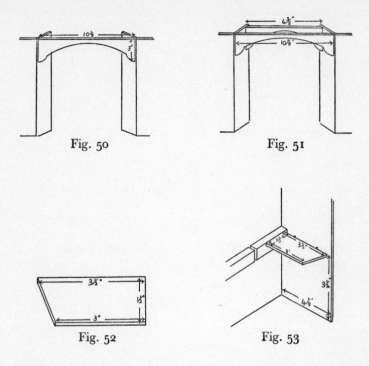

Fig. 50

Fig. 51

Fig. 52

Fig. 53

The next parts to make are the supports for the floors of the second- and third-storey boxes. Cut four pieces of plywood, $3\frac{1}{2}''$ along one side, $3''$ along another, and $1\frac{1}{2}''$ along the side at right angles to these. (See Fig. 52.)

Into the longest edge ($3\frac{1}{2}''$) of one of the pieces drive two veneer-pins : nip off their heads and press the pins against one of the $9''$ by $4\frac{1}{8}''$ sections so that the top surface of the $3\frac{1}{2}''$ by $3''$ by $1\frac{1}{2}''$ piece is level with the upper surface of the first side-wall

83

support above the stage floor with the $1\frac{1}{2}''$ edge tight against it. (See Fig. 53.)

Make holes at the dents and fit the piece in. Then do the same with another of the four pieces—this time level with and against the side-wall support above the last. (See Fig. 54.)

Do the same with the remaining two pieces on the $9\frac{1}{16}''$ by $4\frac{1}{8}''$ section on the other side of the stage.

Now cut another four pieces, each measuring $4\frac{1}{8}''$ along one side, $3\frac{5}{8}''$ along another, and $1\frac{9}{16}''$ along the side at right angles to these. (See Fig. 55.)

These four pieces are the floors proper of the boxes and rest on the supports already made and fitted. (See Figs. 56 and 57.)

For the floors of the second and third storeys between the side walls and the $9\frac{1}{16}''$ by $4\frac{1}{4}''$ inner walls parallel to them, cut four pieces each measuring $4\frac{1}{4}''$ by $1\frac{3}{4}''$. These will rest on the supports on the side walls (see Fig. 58), but you may need additional supports to prevent the floors from tipping in. Two veneer-pins tapped into the $9\frac{1}{16}''$ by $4\frac{1}{4}''$ walls on a level with and opposite each side-wall support, one at the front and one at the back, will provide sufficient support. (See Fig. 59.)

84

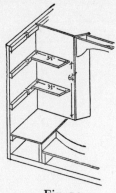

Fig. 54

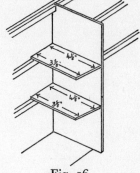

Fig. 56

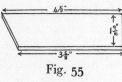

Fig. 55

Fig. 57

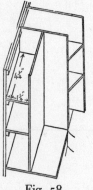

Fig. 58

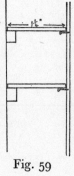

Fig. 59

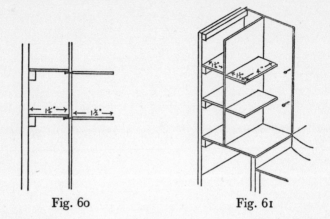

Fig. 60   Fig. 61

The floors of the second- and third-storey galleries remain to be made and fitted, and these will need supports as well. First cut four pieces, each measuring 4″ by $1\frac{1}{2}$″. Into one of the long edges of each knock in two veneer-pins—one near each corner. Nip off their heads so that about $\frac{1}{8}$″ remains protruding and then press the pins against the $9\frac{1}{16}$″ by $4\frac{1}{4}$″ inner walls so that the upper surfaces are level with the bottom surfaces of the floors last fitted. Make holes at the dents and fit them on. (See Fig. 60.)

At the same heights knock in pins into the $9\frac{1}{16}$″ by $3\frac{5}{8}$″ walls, close to the inner vertical edges. (See Fig. 61.)

For the floors themselves cut four pieces, each measuring $4\frac{1}{4}$″ by $2\frac{1}{4}$″, and these will rest on the supports already in position. (See Fig. 62.)

86

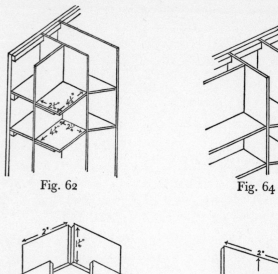

Fig. 62

Fig. 64

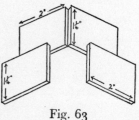

Fig. 63

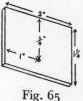

Fig. 65

The fronts of the boxes and side galleries are made
of plywood fixed at right angles into the floors.
For the boxes of the second and third storeys you
need four pieces, each 2″ by 1¼″.   (See Fig. 63.)

Into the middle of the inner edges of each floor
drive a veneer-pin and nip off its head so that
about ⅛″ is left protruding.   (See Fig. 64.)

Now make a hole in each front section, half-way
along the 2″ side and ¾″ in.   (See Fig. 65.)

Then fit the front sections over the pins so that the larger area of each piece is above the pin. (See Fig. 66.)

Following the same method fix fronts on to the second- and third-storey side galleries—each of these measuring $4\frac{1}{4}''$ by $1\frac{1}{4}''$. (See Fig. 67.)

This leaves the fronts for the stage-level boxes and side galleries. For the latter cut two pieces measuring $4\frac{1}{4}''$ by $2''$. Knock a veneer-pin into the middle of one of the long edges of each and press it down on the auditorium floor. Make a hole at the dent and fit the piece in. (See Fig. 68.)

Two pieces measuring $2''$ by $\frac{3}{4}''$ by $\frac{11}{16}''$ (see Fig. 69) fit in the same way in front of the stage-level boxes, the shorter vertical edges being nearer the back of the stage. (See Fig. 70.)

Doorways leading into the boxes and side galleries should now be cut. These can be done in the same way as those suggested for the Elizabethan Theatre, Fig. 30, on page 32. First remove the $9\frac{1}{16}''$ by $4\frac{1}{4}''$ walls and the floors and supports fixed to them : then cut three openings in each—each doorway being $1\frac{7}{8}''$ high and $\frac{3}{4}''$ across. The first doorway is at the bottom of each wall, with one side $3\frac{1}{4}''$ from the edge nearest the front of the model. (See Fig. 71.)

88

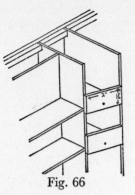

Fig. 66

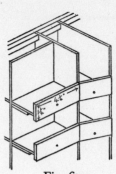

Fig. 67

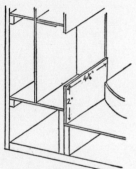

Fig. 68

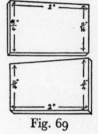

Fig. 69

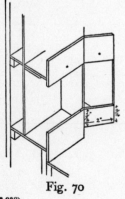

Fig. 70

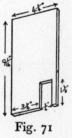

Fig. 71

Directly above, cut two more openings in each wall, the bottoms being on a level with the second- and third-storey floors—i.e. $3\frac{3}{8}''$ and $6\frac{3}{8}''$ from the bottom of the walls. (See Fig. 72.)

Remove the $9\frac{1}{16}''$ by $3\frac{5}{8}''$ walls and cut three openings of the same size ($1\frac{7}{8}''$ by $\frac{3}{4}''$) and at the same heights (at the bottom, and $3\frac{3}{8}''$ and $6\frac{3}{8}''$ from the bottom) in each wall. The vertical edge of each door nearest the side walls should be $\frac{1}{4}''$ from that edge. (See Fig. 73.)

Replace the walls—first the $9\frac{1}{16}''$ by $3\frac{5}{8}''$ (Fig. 74) and then the $9\frac{1}{16}''$ by $4\frac{1}{4}''$ one (Fig. 75)—and the supports, floors and front sections (Fig. 76).

Now remove the two walls which support the arch nearer the front of the stage ($9\frac{1}{16}''$ by $2\frac{3}{4}''$). In the middle of the bottom of each cut an opening measuring $2\frac{1}{2}''$ high by $1\frac{1}{4}''$ across—but keep the little piece which you have cut out. (See Fig. 77.)

Next saw off two small strips, $2\frac{1}{2}''$ by $\frac{1}{2}''$, and fix these alongside the vertical edges of the openings nearer the centre of the stage : this can be done by leaving about $\frac{1}{8}''$ of pin protruding from one of the longer ($2\frac{1}{2}''$) sides which can then fit into a hole in the wall itself. (See Fig. 78.)

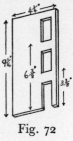

Fig. 72

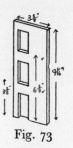

Fig. 73

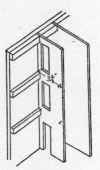

Fig. 74

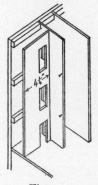

Fig. 75

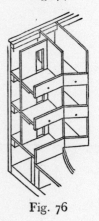

Fig. 76

Fig. 77

91

Cut two strips of canvas, glue one side of each and stick half on to the 2½" by ½" piece and half on to the cut-out doorway piece that you have kept. (See Figs. 79 and 80.)

The walls will then look as in Fig. 81.

The theatre is now complete except for some areas of roofing and shielding (which are not essential, but which are later explained) and for the machinery

Fig. 78

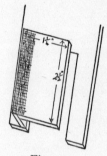

Fig. 79

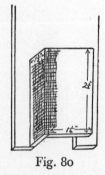

Fig. 80

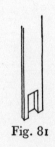

Fig. 81

92

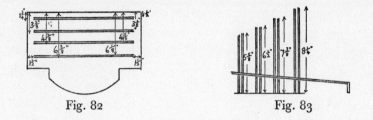

Fig. 82   Fig. 83

for moving scenery. The latter is done by sliding
flats along grooves cut in the stage floor. To make
the grooves, remove the stage floor and with a
pencil draw on the upper surface pairs of lines
$\frac{1}{4}''$ apart running across parallel to the back wall.
These lines begin and end $1\frac{1}{2}''$ in from the sides of
the floor with the back line of each pair being at the
following distances from the back of the stage itself:
$1\frac{1}{2}''$, $3\frac{1}{8}''$, $4\frac{5}{8}''$, $6\frac{1}{4}''$.

Using a wide-bladed saw, cut along each of the
lines so that you finally have eight grooves altogether.
(See Fig. 82.)

The flats to slide along these can be made from
stiff cardboard of a thickness that will allow them to
move easily in the grooves. Each flat should be
$1\frac{3}{4}''$ wide, but there will be four different heights
to give the effect of distance :

1. Four pieces of cardboard $8\frac{1}{4}''$ by $1\frac{3}{4}''$
2. Four pieces of cardboard $7\frac{3}{8}''$ by $1\frac{3}{4}''$
3. Four pieces of cardboard $6\frac{1}{2}''$ by $1\frac{3}{4}''$
4. Four pieces of cardboard $5\frac{5}{8}''$ by $1\frac{3}{4}''$

93

Place these in the grooves, a pair of each height opposite each other on either side of the stage. The highest flats should be in the pair of grooves nearest the front of the stage, the lowest in those nearest the back. From the side they will look as in Fig. 83. With pairs of grooves it means that when one series of flats representing a particular scene is slid away another scene is already in position.

These miniature flats can be painted—or you can pin or stick paper on them on which you can paint—to represent various scenes such as a garden, the parlour of an inn or the throne room of a palace. Perhaps paper superimposed is better because you can then cut the inner edges to whatever shapes you wish. A woodland setting is shown in the photograph facing page 56.

In addition to flats, borders are necessary not only to prevent spectators from seeing the tops of the flats but also to give the effect of sky or ceilings. These borders have to hang above the stage between the tops of the flats, and so a system of ' flying ' has to be made.

First of all cut two lengths of $\frac{7}{8}''$ lath-wood, each measuring $1' 6\frac{7}{8}''$. Into the upper surface of the top supports fixed to the side walls drive four veneer-pins ; two of them $5\frac{15}{16}''$ from the front of the model and two $2\frac{15}{16}''$ from the inside of the back wall. Nip off their heads and then make holes in the lath-wood pieces so that when fixed in position across the stage the front edge of one will be $5\frac{1}{2}''$

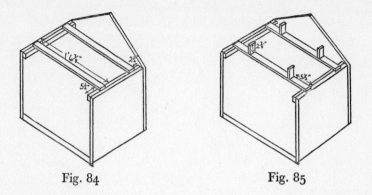

Fig. 84   Fig. 85

from the front of the model and the back edge of the other $2\frac{1}{2}''$ from the inside of the back wall. (See Fig. 84.)

Next cut four pieces of $\frac{7}{8}''$ lath-wood, each $2\frac{7}{8}''$ long. Knock a pin into one of the short edges of each and nip off its head to leave about $\frac{1}{4}''$ protruding. Press these pieces down on the 1' $6\frac{7}{8}''$ cross lengths so that, when fixed into corresponding holes, one will be $5\frac{1}{2}''$ from one end of the cross lengths and at right angles to it, another the same distance from the other end, and the remaining two directly behind them on the other cross length. (See Fig. 85.)

Now cut two more pieces of lath-wood, each $9\frac{5}{8}''$ long. Remove the four pieces last fixed ($2\frac{7}{8}''$ by $\frac{7}{8}''$) and into the other short edge of each drive a pin (that is the edge opposite the one with a pin in already). Nip off the heads, replace the four

95

pieces, and then place the $9\frac{5}{8}''$ lengths over the $2\frac{7}{8}''$ pieces from back to front, the front end of each $9\frac{5}{8}''$ length being flush with the front end of the support beneath. Make holes at the dents and fit the $9\frac{5}{8}''$ lengths on firmly. (See Fig. 86.)

On the underside of the $9\frac{5}{8}''$ pieces will be fitted pulleys—or $\frac{1}{2}''$ staples—to take strings which, in turn, will hold little rods, which, in turn, will hold the borders. Remove the $9\frac{5}{8}''$ lengths and turn them over. Down the middle of one, and slightly to one side of the middle of the other, knock in a row of little pulleys or staples at the following distances from the front : $2\frac{1}{4}''$, $4\frac{1}{2}''$, $6\frac{1}{8}''$, $7\frac{5}{8}''$, $9''$ and two at $9\frac{1}{2}''$. (See Fig. 87.) Along the one with the pulleys or staples slightly off the middle line knock in another row. (See Fig. 88.)

Replace these sections. From a length of wire, about $\frac{1}{10}''$ thick, cut one piece $6\frac{1}{2}''$ long and six $9\frac{1}{2}''$ long. About $\frac{1}{4}''$ in from each end of each piece cut out—preferably with a hacksaw—a small nick. (See Fig. 89.)

On the outside of the side wall nearest the $9\frac{5}{8}''$ lath-wood piece with the double row of staples stick in seven drawing pins—but not right in. (See Fig. 90.)

Now take two spools of string, or, better still, thread of two different colours, and break or cut seven lengths of one colour, each about 2' long and seven lengths of another colour, each about 3' long.

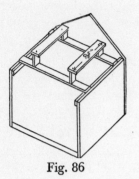

Fig. 86

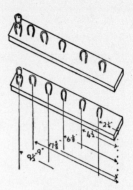

Fig. 87

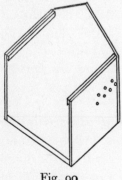

Fig. 88

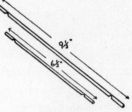

Fig. 89

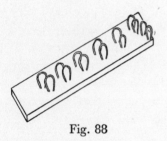

Fig. 90

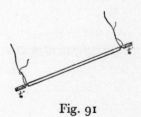

Fig. 91

97

Tie the end of one of the 2′ lengths round one of the pieces of wire at the nick, and the end of one of the 3′ lengths at the other nick. (See Fig. 91.)

Do the same with all the other lengths on the other wires. Pass the free end of the 3′ thread on the 6½″ wire through the pulley or staple nearest the front end of the 9⅝″ lath-wood piece with the single row of pulleys or staples : then pass it through the outer staple of the first pair on the other 9⅝″ piece ; and so over the top outside edge of the side wall with the drawing-pins and round the shaft of the first pin.

Then pass the free end of the 2′ length of thread on that same wire through the pulley or staple at the front of the inner row of the 9⅝″ piece, over the top of the side wall and round the shaft of the same drawing-pin. Do the same thing with all the other threads and wires. (See Fig. 92.)

When you have finished you will be able to raise and lower any of the wire ' battens ', each end independently, from outside the model (the end of the battens being identified, of course, by the different coloured threads ; and the position of the batten by the position of the drawing-pin round which the threads are wound).

The borders themselves can now be fixed to the battens : these can be made of paper or cloth and tied to or stuck on to the wires. Four borders are necessary to conceal the tops of the four pairs of

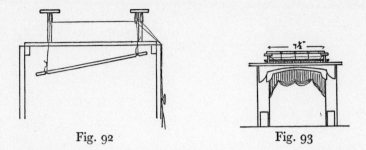

Fig. 92   Fig. 93

flats in use at a time. They should be about the same length as the wires ($9\frac{1}{2}''$ to $10''$) and about $2\frac{3}{4}''$ deep. Fix these on to the second 'batten' from the front and on the next three. The last two battens are best kept for hanging back-cloths or back-drops. These again can be made of paper or cloth and painted to represent the horizon of an outdoor scene or the back wall of an interior set. The size can be about $7''$ across and $5\frac{1}{4}''$ deep.

I have suggested two back-drops because one can be pulled up out of sight while one series of flats are slid off into the wings. The first wire batten should hold the curtain that cuts off the front or 'apron' stage from the back. It is shorter than the others so that it can be pulled up higher. For the curtain use a thin but rich-looking material, $6\frac{1}{2}''$ across and $8''$ deep. To loop it across when it is raised you can pass three or four threads through it from top to bottom, the free ends of which can be wound round the shafts of drawing-pins fixed into a narrow strip of wood placed over the $9\frac{5}{8}''$ pieces above the first set of pulleys or staples. (See Fig. 93.)

99

The theatre is now complete. If, however, you want to roof it and cover the front of the side galleries and the sections below them and the auditorium floor, it is very easily done with stiff cardboard. First cut a triangular piece $1' 7\frac{1}{4}''$ base and $5\frac{1}{2}''$ height and place this up against the front of the lath-wood pieces. (See Fig. 94.)

Then cut two pieces of cardboard, each $1' 3''$ by $11\frac{3}{8}''$, and place these along the top of the side walls and over the back wall to form a sloping roof. If they do not stay up firmly you can always tap in a few veneer-pins to hold them on the side walls. (See Fig. 95.)

A ridge piece—also of cardboard—$1' 3\frac{1}{2}''$ long by $2''$ can be bent along the middle at the right angle and placed over the join of the roof pieces. (See Fig. 96.)

Ceilings of cardboard cut to the shape as in Fig. 97 will fit over the third-storey boxes and side galleries.

Another possible addition is a set of seats for the side galleries. These can be made from small strips of plywood pinned together. You will need six of these. (See Fig. 98 and also Scale Drawing D).

The shielding pieces can be made of cardboard, two $1' 1\frac{5}{8}''$ by $4\frac{1}{8}''$ and one $11\frac{1}{2}''$ by $2''$, and fixed at the front of the model by veneer- or drawing-pins. (See Fig. 99.)

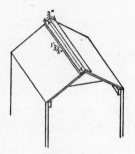

Fig. 94

Fig. 95

Fig. 96

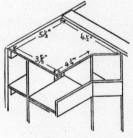

Fig. 97

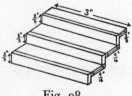

Fig. 98

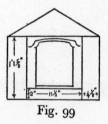

Fig. 99

101

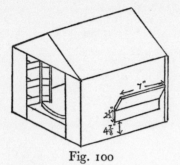

Fig. 100

Finally, if you want to move your model actors without putting your hands over the stage itself, it is possible to cut out a section of one, or both, side walls. In Fig. 100 you can see a section which is hinged and can be held open by a latch.

For painting the model, suggestions on the better kinds of media are on page 54.

The colours, again, are up to you. One possible scheme is to paint all main walls, roofs, shielding sections and lath-wood flies white. Leave the stage-floor in natural wood—and all the other floors as well. Blue can be used for the inside walls of the boxes and side galleries. The front vertical edge of the stage, the fronts of the boxes and side galleries, the stage-doors, the walls above them and the arches look well panelled in blue and gold. With this particular colour scheme the front curtain could be made of a crimson or gold material.

This theatre can be used for any kind of play, although it lends itself best, of course, to those written in the eighteenth century (by Gay, Goldsmith, Sheridan, etc.).

To help you in your building there are these scale drawings of the theatre.

Fig. A   Plan of the Base
Fig. B   Plan at Auditorium-floor Level
Fig. C   Plan at Stage-floor Level
Fig. D   Front Elevation
Fig. E   Cross Section
          and also in proportion, but not to scale
Fig. F   Isometric Projection

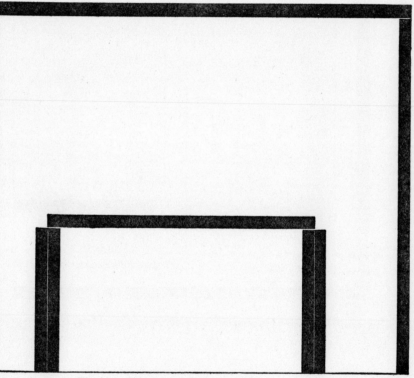

Fig. A   Plan of the Base.   Scale 1 : 4

Fig. B Plan at Auditorium-floor Level. Scale 1 : 4

104

Modern theatre

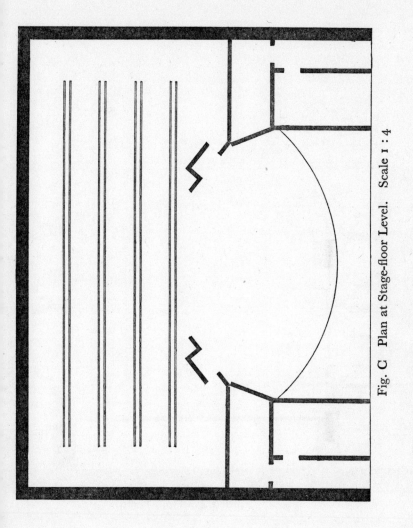

Fig. C   Plan at Stage-floor Level.   Scale 1 : 4

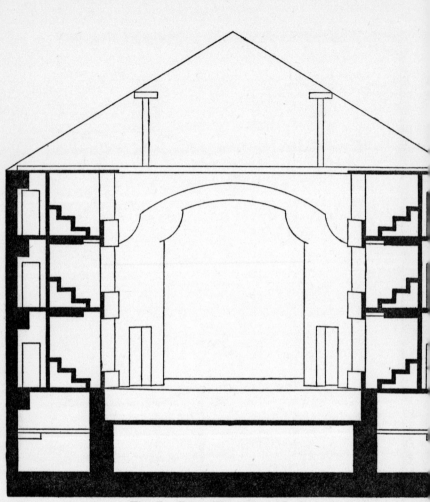

Fig. D   Front Elevation.   Scale 1 : 4

106

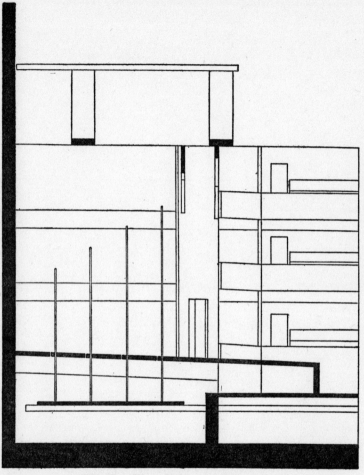

Fig. E   Cross Section.   Scale 1 : 4

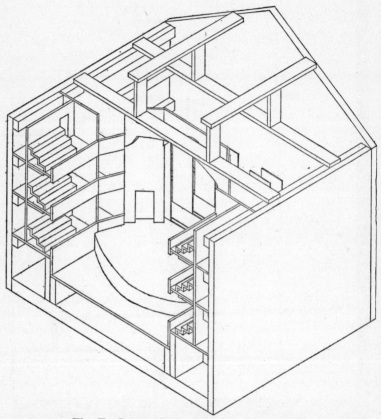

Fig. F   Isometric Projection.   Not to scale

THE MODERN THEATRE

Materials required :

		from
Plywood	10 sq. ft.	7s to 8s 6d
1″ Hard-wood	3 sq. ft.	
½″ Hard-wood	2½ sq. ft.	
⅞″ Lath-wood	20 ft.	1s 8d to 3s 4d
Wire	17 ft.	9d
1″ Oval nails	4 oz.	7d
¾″ Veneer/Panel pins	1 packet	6d
Screw-eyes	100	2s 6d
(½″ Staples)	(4 oz.)	(9d)
Paint (Emulsion/Oil/Poster)		
Thread	2 reels	
Drawing-pins	1 packet	

Total   from 11s 6d to 16s 3d

Tools required :

Hammer, saw (for hard-wood), tenon-saw (for plywood and lath-wood), wire-cutters, pliers, ruler (with $\frac{1}{8}$s and $\frac{1}{16}$s), pencil, compasses, set-square or triangle, sandpaper, knife or razor blade, paint brushes. (Additional tools—not essential : plane, fret-saw, shooting-board, hack-saw, spirit-level.)

This model of a modern theatre is the easiest of the three to build ; in design it is less complicated than either the Elizabethan or eighteenth-century theatre.

The back wall is the first part to make and this should be of 1″-thick wood, measuring 1′ 2½″ by 1′ 10⅝″. (See Fig. 1.)

Don't forget, however, to sandpaper off all edges after you have cut a piece of wood or plywood.

Now cut out the base of the model—again of 1″ wood rather than ½″—1′ 1½″ by 1′ 3⅝″. (See Fig. 2.)

Into one of the shorter edges (1′ 1½″) drive three 1″ oval nails about a quarter-way in, and nip off their heads. (See Fig. 3 and also Elizabethan Theatre, Figs. 2 and 3.)

Now press the headless nails against the back wall so that the bottom surface of the base is level with the bottom edge of the back wall, leaving ½″ of the back wall protruding from either corner of the base. (See Fig. 4.)

Make holes where the headless nails dented the back wall—make the holes by driving into the back wall at the three dents a 1″ oval nail. (You can use the same nail for this purpose over and over again—provided it doesn't get bent). Then fit the base on to the back wall. (See Fig. 5.)

For the two side walls of the model saw two rectangular pieces of ½″ wood, each measuring 1′ 3⅞″ by 1′ 1½″. (See Fig. 6.)

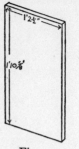

Fig. 1

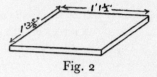

Fig. 2

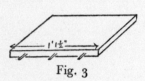

Fig. 3

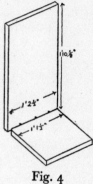

Fig. 4

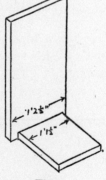

Fig. 5

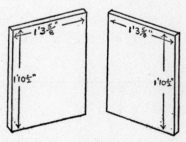

Fig. 6

III

Lay these pieces down flat and on the surface of each draw a line parallel with the long (1′ 10½″) sides and 8¾″ from one of them. Call the top corner of the side from which you took that measurement ' a '; mark a point ' b ' 1′ ⅜″ from the bottom of the line you have drawn; another point ' c ' on the same line 1″ from the top; and a point ' d ' 1′ 1½″ from the bottom of the other long side. (See Fig. 7.)

Join ' a ' to ' c ', and ' b ' to ' d '; and saw out the area shaded in Fig. 8.

Into each of the long (1′ 3⅞″) edges of the base drive three 1″ oval nails and nip off their heads. (See Fig. 9.)

Press one of the side walls against those decapitated nails on one side of the base so that the vertical back edge (1′ 10½″) of the side wall fits against the back wall into the ½″ space. Make holes at the dents in the side wall and fit it on to the base. (See Fig. 10.)

(You may also find it useful to knock a nail into each side wall high up on the back edge to fit through a corresponding hole in the back wall.)

Do the same with the other side wall on the opposite side. (See Fig. 11.)

You will now find that the top edge of the back wall is ⅛″ higher than the highest part of the side

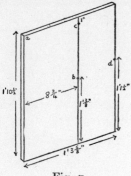

Fig. 7

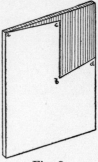

Fig. 8

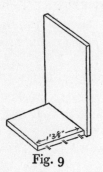

Fig. 9

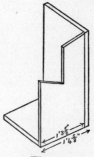

Fig. 10

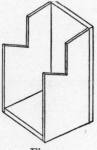

Fig. 11

Fig. 12a

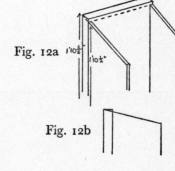

Fig. 12b

walls. With a plane and/or tough sandpaper angle the top of the back wall to meet the top of the side walls. (See Figs. 12a and 12b.)

Having made the main walls, you might as well now do the roofs and the front wall between them. For the roof over the higher part of the theatre cut a piece of plywood measuring 1' 2¾" by 10½". This will rest on the top of the back wall and on the higher parts of the side walls. You can, however, fix it on firmly by knocking into the top edges of the side walls two or four ¾" veneer (or 'panel') pins which, when decapitated, can fit into corresponding holes just inside the sides of the roof. (See Fig. 13.)

The next piece is the vertical front wall below that roof. For this cut a piece of plywood, 1' 2½" by 9½", and from two corresponding corners remove a small rectangular section, ½" along the long side and ⅜" along the short. (See Figs. 14a and 14b.)

This will then fit against the vertical edges of the side walls and over the upward sloping tops of the side walls at their lowest point. (See Fig. 15.)

Again, a veneer-pin driven into each of the side walls at point 'x' (in Fig. 15), decapitated and fitted into a corresponding hole in the plywood front wall will hold the piece firmly in position.

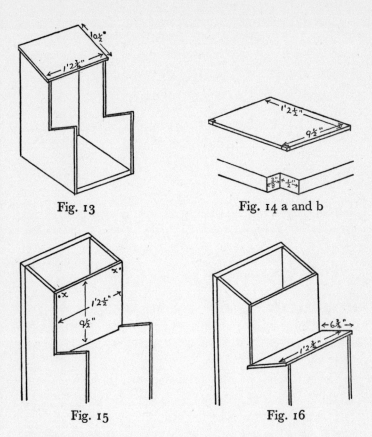

Fig. 13

Fig. 14 a and b

Fig. 15

Fig. 16

For the roof over the front part of the theatre cut
a piece of plywood, 1′ 2¾″ by 6¾″, and this will
rest on the tops of the upward sloping side walls
with one long edge against the front wall just fitted.
(See Fig. 16.)

Now remove the vertical front wall (1′ 2½″ by 9½″).
Cut a piece of plywood measuring 8¼″ by 2″.

115

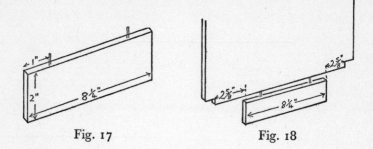

Fig. 17   Fig. 18

About 1″ in from each end of one of the long edges
drive a veneer-pin half-way in and nip off its head.
(See Fig. 17 and also Elizabethan Theatre, Figs. 3
and 21.)

Press this piece against the edge of the front wall
which has the cut corners so that each end of the
$8\frac{1}{4}″$ piece is $2\frac{5}{8}″$ in from the end of the 1′ $1\frac{1}{2}″$ edge.
(See Fig. 18.)

Make holes at the two dents, with another veneer-
pin, and fit on the $8\frac{1}{4}″$ piece.   (See Fig. 19.)

Now remove the lower roof (1′ $2\frac{3}{4}″$ by $6\frac{3}{4}″$).   Cut
two pieces of plywood each measuring 1′ $1\frac{1}{2}″$ by
$3\frac{5}{8}″$.   (See Fig. 20.)

On the surface of each of these pieces mark points
' a ' and ' b ' $2\frac{1}{2}″$ along the short sides : draw a
line parallel with the short sides $1\frac{1}{8}″$ in from each

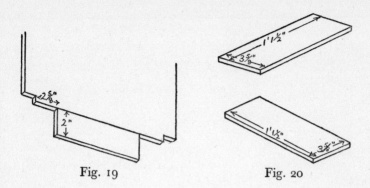

Fig. 19   Fig. 20

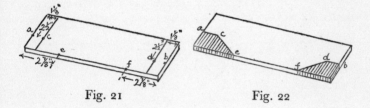

Fig. 21   Fig. 22

of them ; on these lines mark points ' c ' and ' d '
also $2\frac{1}{2}''$ along ; and on the long side nearer these
points mark two more ' e ' and ' f ' $2\frac{7}{8}''$ in from each
end. (See Fig. 21.)

Join ' a ', ' c ' and ' e ' ; and ' b ', ' d ' and ' f '.
Saw off the shaded area as in Fig. 22.

This will leave you with two octagonal pieces of the
shape as in Fig. 23.

Now cut four little pieces of plywood, each measuring $1\frac{7}{8}''$ by $\frac{3}{4}''$. (See Fig. 24.)

117

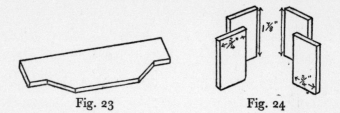

Fig. 23   Fig. 24

On one of the long sides of each little piece mark
a point $\frac{1}{8}''$ from one end, and another $\frac{3}{8}''$ from the
other end ; join these two points to the nearer
corner of the opposite long side. Then cut off the
shaded portion as in Fig. 25.

This will leave you with four pieces of the shape
as in Fig. 26. And, into the short edge with the
less acute angle, drive a veneer-pin.

Fit one of these pieces into the underside of the
lower roof ($1'\ 2\frac{3}{4}''$ by $6\frac{3}{4}''$) with the pin $\frac{1}{2}''$ in from
the back—or lower—edge and $1\frac{5}{8}''$ in from one side.
(See Fig. 27.)

Do the same with another piece on the other side
of the roof. (See Fig. 28.)

The other two pieces fit into the underside of the
roof behind those already in position—$1\frac{5}{8}''$ in from
the sides as before, but $4''$ in from the back edge.
(See Fig. 29.)

Now take the two octagonal pieces (Fig. 23) and,
at an angle, drive a pin into each close to the two

118

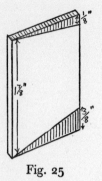

Fig. 25

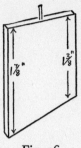

Fig. 26

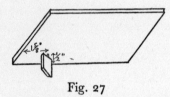

Fig. 27

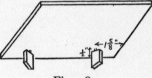

Fig. 28

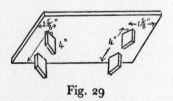

Fig. 29

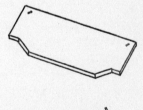

Fig. 30 a and b

corners which are at right angles. (See Figs. 30a and 30b.)

Press the long edge of one against the underside of the roof so that it lies $2\frac{3}{4}''$ from the back edge and $\frac{1}{2}''$ in from each side. The first two supports fitted will then hold that octagonal piece out from the roof at an angle. (See Figs. 31a and 31b.)

The other octagonal piece fits behind that with its long edge $6\frac{1}{4}''$ from the back edge of the roof. (See Figs. 32a and 32b.)

These attachments to the ceiling over the auditorium are called 'baffles'. Their most important use in a theatre is to reflect sound—but they also provide concealed places for fixing lights to throw beams on to the stage itself. Lights placed in the auditorium and used for the stage are called 'front-of-house' or F.O.H. lights. The 'baffle' near the front of this model can be used for that purpose. A wire fixed across the second pair of supports fitted can hold miniature lamps which cannot be seen from the front.

Now it is time to get on with the stage itself. First of all, however, a small area of auditorium floor must be made and fitted. The supports for this floor will be of $\frac{7}{8}''$ lath-wood (the kind used for garden trellis-work and for plastering). Cut four lengths, each $5\frac{3}{4}''$ long. Into one of the long edges

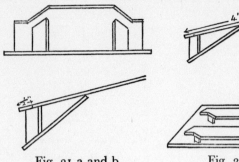

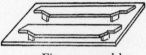

Fig. 31 a and b   Fig. 32 a and b

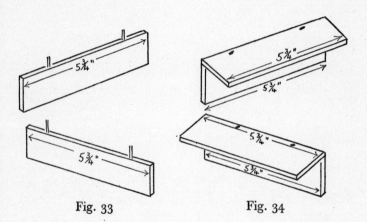

Fig. 33   Fig. 34

of two of these pieces drive two veneer-pins and nip off their heads.   (See Fig. 33.)

Then press the other two pieces against these pins at right angles so that one long edge of each is flush with one of the long sides beneath.   Make holes at the dents and fit on.   (See Fig. 34.)

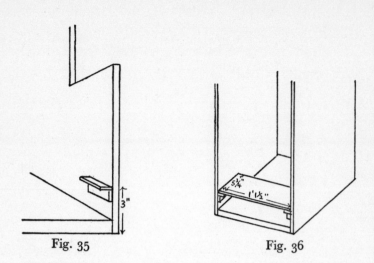

Fig. 35   Fig. 36

Now place one of the double-pieces against the inside of one of the side walls so that the upper surface of the top part is 3″ above the bottom of the base. Knock two veneer-pins into the lower part and through into the side wall. (See Fig. 35.)

Do the same with the other double-support on the opposite side wall. Then cut a piece of plywood measuring 1′ 1½″ by 5¾″. This will then rest on those supports across the front of the model. (See Fig. 36.)

The supports for the stage floor itself are made in the same way as the others—from four pieces of ⅞″ lath-wood fitted together to form two double-pieces, but their length this time is 9½″ each. (See Fig. 37.)

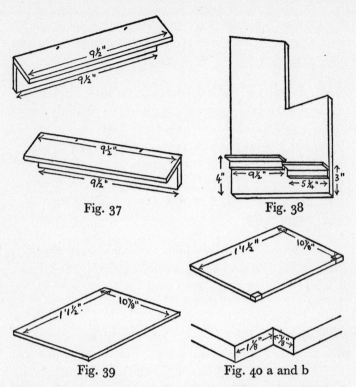

Fig. 37

Fig. 38

Fig. 39

Fig. 40 a and b

They fit on to the inside of the side walls behind and above the supports for the auditorium floor—their upper surfaces being 4″ above the bottom of the base. (See Fig. 38.)

For the floor itself use, if possible, a piece of mahogany-finished plywood measuring 1′ 1½″ by 10⅞″. (See Fig. 39.)

From two corresponding corners cut out a small rectangle, 1⅛″ from the long side and ⅞″ from the short side. (See Figs. 40a and 40b.)

Place this over the auditorium floor, resting on the side supports with the back edge against the inside of the back wall. (See Fig. 41.)

The difference in height between the auditorium floor and the stage floor will be $1''$. For the vertical edge cut one piece of plywood, $11\frac{5}{8}''$ by $1''$; two pieces, $1\frac{1}{8}''$ by $1''$; and two pieces, $\frac{11}{16}''$ by $1''$. Into the front edges of the stage floor knock four or five pins in the long ($11\frac{1}{4}''$) edge, two into each of the $1\frac{1}{8}''$ edges, and one into each of the $\frac{7}{8}''$ edges. (See Fig. 42.)

Press the five $1''$-high pieces against the headless pins (which should project about $\frac{1}{8}''$ from the edges), make holes at the dents and fit them on. (See Fig. 43.)

The next pieces to make are the walls which cut off the stage and the wings from the audience. For these cut two pieces of plywood, each measuring $7\frac{3}{4}''$ by $1\frac{1}{8}''$; and two measuring $7\frac{3}{4}''$ by $2\frac{1}{4}''$. Into one of the short edges of each knock a veneer-pin. (See Fig. 44.)

Take one of the narrower sections and press it down on to one of the $1\frac{1}{8}''$ by $1''$ vertical front pieces. Make a hole at the dent and fit it on. (See Fig. 45.)

Do the same with the other narrower piece at the other side. Then fit one of the broader pieces on

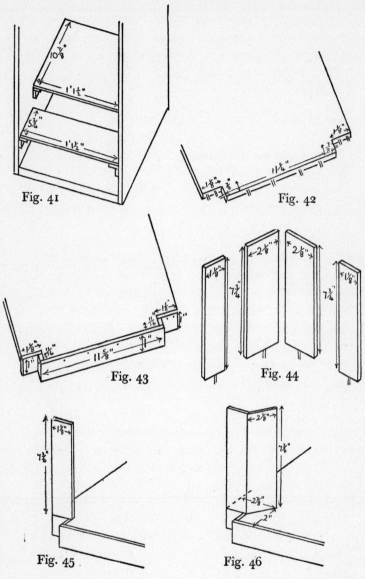

Fig. 41

Fig. 42

Fig. 43

Fig. 44

Fig. 45

Fig. 46

to the stage floor so that one vertical edge meets the front inner vertical edge of one of the narrower pieces, while the other vertical edge is 2″ from the front of the stage and 2⅛″ from the side. (See Fig. 46.)

Do the same with the other broader piece on the other side. Now you will find that the outer vertical edges of the broader pieces will not fit tight against the inner vertical edges of the narrower pieces. This is easily remedied, however, by sandpapering off the outer vertical edges of the broader pieces at an angle. (See Figs. 47a and 47b.)

The last piece of construction (apart from those to do with the machinery) is a kind of proscenium arch. For this cut a piece of plywood measuring 8¼″ by 5¾″. Lay this flat : on its surface draw a line parallel with the long sides ⅝″ in from one of them ; and a line parallel with the short sides ½″ in from each end. Call the intersections of these lines ' a ' and ' b '. (See Fig. 48.)

At these two points draw an arc to round off the right angle so that the curves meet the straight lines about 1″ to 1¼″ from ' a ' and ' b '. With a fret-saw (or some other cutting tool) remove the shaded area as in Fig. 49.

This will leave you with your arch, and into the bottom edge of each ' leg ' drive a veneer-pin. (See Fig. 50.)

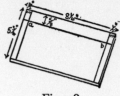

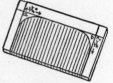

Fig. 47 a and b   Fig. 48

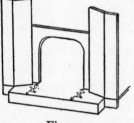

Fig. 49   Fig. 50

Fig. 51

Now fit the arch on to the stage floor behind the
two broad walls, each outer vertical edge being
$2\frac{5}{8}''$ in from the sides and $2\frac{1}{4}''$ from the front.   (See
Fig. 51.)

If you wish you can leave the construction of the
model at that.   However, to change scenery quickly

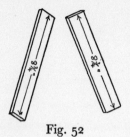

Fig. 52

and to fix up lights you can make use of the high area above the stage floor—called the 'stage tower'. In it a grid can be built up near the ceiling with a fly-rail below and a cat-walk below that for lights. These pieces are best made of $\frac{7}{8}$" lath-wood and fairly thick ($\frac{1}{10}$") wire.

For the 'cat-walk' cut two pieces of lath-wood, each 8$\frac{3}{4}$" long. (See Fig. 52.)

Into one of the long edges of each drive three veneer-pins and nip off their heads. Press these against the side walls so that their upper surfaces are 6$\frac{3}{4}$" above the stage floor. (See Fig. 53.)

Make holes at the dents and fit them in. Then cut another piece of lath-wood, 1' 1" long. This will go across the stage with its ends resting on the 8$\frac{3}{4}$" pieces—the long front edge being about $\frac{1}{4}$" in from the short front edges of the 8$\frac{3}{4}$" pieces. (See Fig. 54.)

From your length or roll of wire cut six little pieces, each 2" long ; two pieces, each 7$\frac{1}{2}$" long ; two pieces, each 8$\frac{1}{2}$" long ; and two pieces, each 12$\frac{3}{4}$" long.

128

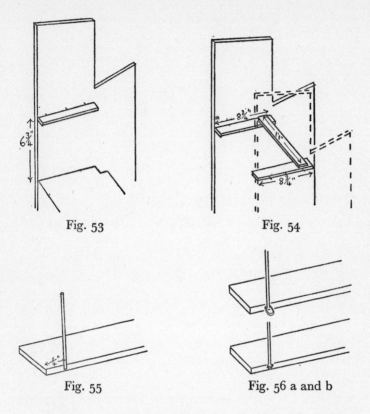

Fig. 53

Fig. 54

Fig. 55

Fig. 56 a and b

Remove one of the $8\frac{3}{4}''$ lath-wood pieces. Place one of the 2″ wires against its inner edge, one end being flush with the bottom of the piece and about $\frac{1}{4}''$ in from the end of the lath-wood piece which is next to the back wall.   (See Fig. 55.)

Take a $\frac{1}{2}''$ staple and knock it into the inner edge of the lath-wood piece to hold the 2″ wire firmly upright.   (See Figs. 56a and 56b.)

Do the same with another 2″ wire, this time $2\frac{1}{4}″$ from the other end of the same lath-wood piece. (See Fig. 57.)

Now fix one of the $7\frac{1}{2}″$ wires between the two upright 2″ ones so that it is $\frac{3}{4}″$ above the upper surface of the lath-wood piece. This you can do by bending each end tightly round the uprights. (See Fig. 58.)

The other $7\frac{1}{2}″$ wire fits in the same way above, $1\frac{1}{2}″$ from the top of the support. (See Fig. 59.)

Then, to keep the whole structure taut, bend over the tops of the 2″ wires. (See Fig. 60.)

On the other $8\frac{3}{4}″$ piece fix wires in the same positions —with one difference : the 2″ wire at the end near the front should be $1\frac{1}{4}″$ in from the end (not $2\frac{1}{4}″$) —the long cross wires being the two $8\frac{1}{2}″$ ones.

On the 1′ 1″ lath-wood piece fit the 2″ uprights 1″ from each end and use the two $12\frac{3}{4}″$ wires as cross pieces. When the lath-wood pieces are all in position you will have a cat-walk running round three sides of the stage on which you can fit lights in any place you wish.

For the ' flies ' cut three pieces of lath-wood of the same sizes as for the cat-walk (two, $8\frac{3}{4}″$; and one, 1′ 1″). These will fit on the side walls as the others, this time $12\frac{3}{8}″$ above the stage. The trans-

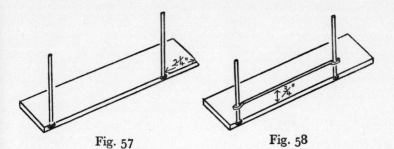

Fig. 57   Fig. 58

Fig. 59   Fig. 60

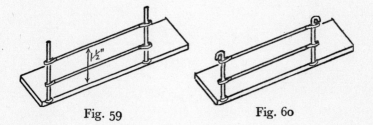

Fig. 61   Fig. 62

verse piece (1′ 1″) you can then fix with wires as you did the other one below—i.e. with two 2″ uprights 1″ from each end and two cross wires, each 12¾″ long, bent round them.

For the fly-rail itself cut a piece of lath-wood 6¾″ long. Drive two veneer-pins into one of its long edges, press them down on the 8¾″ piece, one short vertical edge being flush with one end of the piece beneath, make holes at the dents and fit it on. (See Fig. 61.)

On the lath-wood piece opposite fit on another lath-wood piece 7½″ long. (See Fig. 62.)

Now take the one with the 6¾″ vertical piece again. Into the back of it knock in (but not right in) nine small screw-eyes, or ½″ staples, in a row at equal distances from each other. And into the horizontal piece near the front another screw-eye or staple. (See Fig. 63.)

These screw-eyes or staples will be used for passing through the strings from the grid which will in turn hold ten wire battens. Now the grid itself will be supported by another two 8¾″ lath-wood pieces fixed into the side walls 1′ 4⅜″ above the stage. (See Fig. 64.)

When you have fitted those two supports, cut yet another three more 8¾″ lath-pieces and lay them flat parallel with one another so that the distance between the middle of the first two is 2¾″ and between the second and third 5½″. (See Fig. 65.)

Then cut ten lengths of $\frac{7}{16}$″ lath-wood each 1′ 1″ long, and lay these across the three 8¾″ pieces, the first one being ½″ in from the ends of the 8¾″ pieces

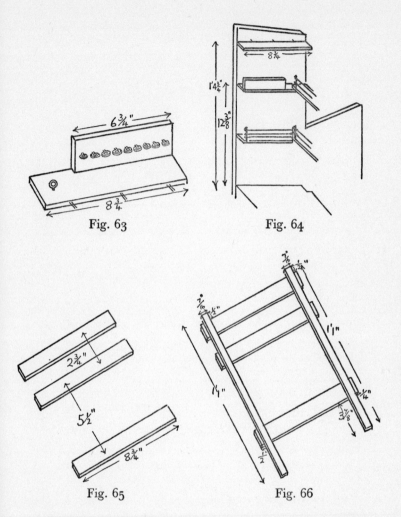

Fig. 63

Fig. 64

Fig. 65

Fig. 66

and the tenth being $\frac{1}{4}''$ in from the other ends. They will project $\frac{1}{2}''$ beyond the long side of the first $8\frac{3}{4}''$ piece and $3\frac{7}{8}''$ beyond the long side of the third $8\frac{3}{4}''$ piece.   (See Fig. 66.)

133

The second $\frac{7}{16}''$ piece will be $1\frac{1}{2}''$ from the first. (See Fig. 67.)

The remaining seven pieces will lie between the second and tenth with about $\frac{1}{4}''$ between one another. (See Fig. 68.)

At each intersection of the $8\frac{3}{4}''$ and $1'\,1''$ pieces knock in a veneer-pin—you will need thirty pins altogether. (See Fig. 69.)

Into the $8\frac{3}{4}''$ pieces at each space put in a small screw-eye or staple—but those in the first and second $8\frac{3}{4}''$ pieces should be slightly to one side. (See Fig. 70.)

Then put in another row into the spaces on the first and second $8\frac{3}{4}''$ pieces. You will need fifty screw-eyes or staples altogether. (See Fig. 71.)

Now turn your grid up the other way and place it over the stage resting on the top side-wall supports. The pieces with double rows of screw-eyes or staples should be above the fly-rail with its row of screw-eyes, and the two $1'\,1''$ which are $1\frac{1}{2}''$ apart should be at the front.

Cut ten pieces of wire, each $9\frac{1}{2}''$ long. These will be the battens. About $\frac{1}{4}''$ in from each end of each piece make a nick—with a hack-saw, if you have one. (See Eighteenth-century Theatre, Fig. 89.) Take two reels of different coloured

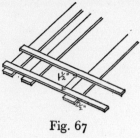

Fig. 67

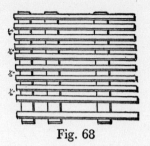

Fig. 68

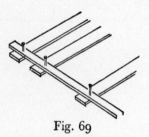

Fig. 69

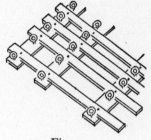

Fig. 70

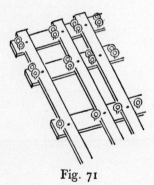

Fig. 71

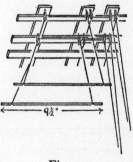

Fig. 72

135

thread and break off ten lengths of one colour, each about $2\frac{1}{2}'$ long, and ten lengths of the other colour, each about $3'$ long. Tie one end of a long thread to one end of one $9\frac{1}{2}''$ wire and pass the other end through the first screw-eye or staple of the single row, then through the first screw-eye farthest away of the next double row, and then through the first screw-eye farthest away of the final double row. Having done this pass the end down through the screw-eye on the floor of the flies below and up and over the top of the side wall. Leave it dangling down the outside of the side wall. Then tie an end of a shorter thread round the other nick in the $9\frac{1}{2}''$ wire and pass the other end through the first free screw-eye of the first double row, through the first free screw-eye of the next double row, down and through the same screw-eye in the fly-floor and up and over the side wall to dangle with the other thread. Then take another $9\frac{1}{2}''$ wire and go through the same process, using the screw-eyes in the next series and the first screw-eye fixed into the back of the fly-rail. (See Fig. 72.)

When you have done the same thing with all the other battens you will have twenty threads dangling down the outside of one side wall. Fix ten drawing-pins fairly high up on that wall, pull each pair of threads to bring each batten up to the grid, and wind the threads round their corresponding drawing-pins. You can then select any batten you want and raise or lower it at will—each end independently by pulling on one coloured thread or the other. (You can see a simplified version of this system in Figs. 91 and 92 of the Eighteenth-century Theatre.)

To connect the stage with the cat-walk, the flies and the grid you can make a ladder from two thin pieces of wood, each 1' 5⅜" high, with rungs made of match-sticks glued across the uprights. (See Fig. 73.)

If you wish to move figures about the stage from outside you can cut out one or two rectangular openings in one or both side walls and hinge doors above them. (See Fig. 74.)

Finally you may wish to shield in the area under the stage from the front; and for this a piece of cardboard, 1' 1½" by 2⅞", pinned across the bottom will do. (See Fig. 75.)

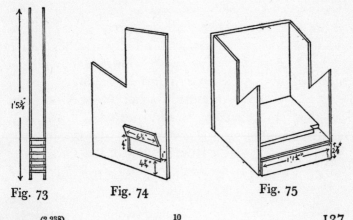

Fig. 73   Fig. 74   Fig. 75

To help you in your building there are these scale drawings of the theatre.

Once again the colours which you use for painting the theatre are up to you, although it is better not to use gloss paint. One suggestion is to paint all the outside walls white, the outside roofs dark grey. The inside side-walls, the lower ceiling, the two angled walls on stage ($7\frac{3}{4}''$ by $2\frac{1}{8}''$) and the piece ($8\frac{1}{4}''$ by $2''$) fixed to the bottom of the front wall can be a very pale pink/orange; the proscenium arch, the two walls ($7\frac{3}{4}''$ by $1\frac{1}{8}''$), the front vertical edge of the stage, and the ' baffles ' all a dark blue-grey. The auditorium floor can be covered with a piece of material or painted—royal blue. For the front curtain a rich piece of material of that same colour would probably look well. Leave the stage as natural wood ; if you pin on a shielding strip paint it white as you did the outside walls. There is no need to paint anything in the ' stage tower '.

138

Fig. A   Plan of the Base.   Scale 1 : 4

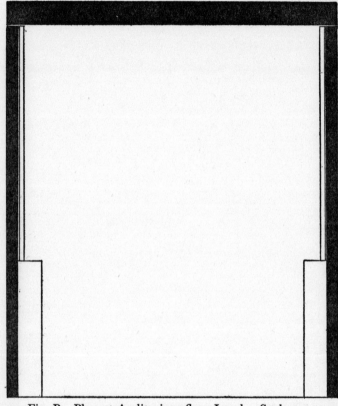

Fig. B   Plan at Auditorium-floor Level.   Scale 1 : 4

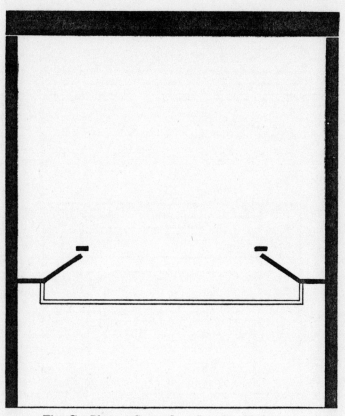

Fig. C   Plan at Stage-floor Level.   Scale 1 : 4

Fig. D   Front Elevation without Roofs
and Front Wall.   Scale 1 : 4

Fig. E   Front Elevation.   Scale 1 : 4

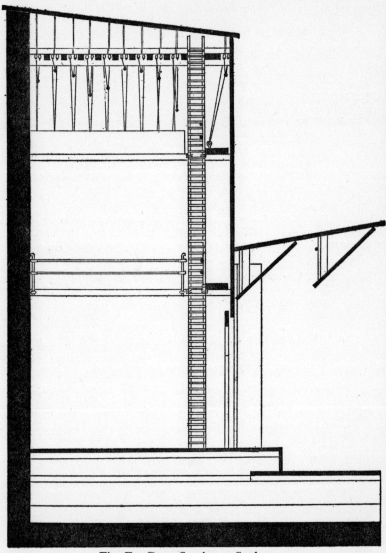

Fig. F   Cross Section.   Scale 1 : 4

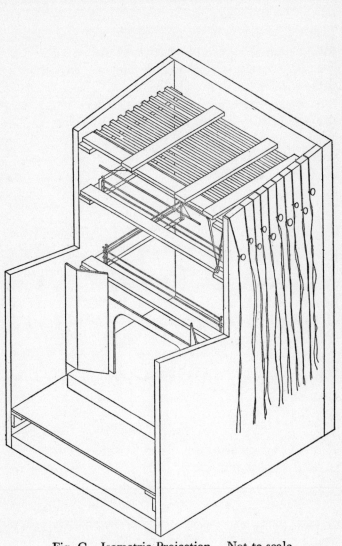

Fig. G   Isometric Projection.   Not to scale

This can mostly be made from cardboard, cut to the various shapes and sizes you require. Flats are the most important items, of course, and most of these should be about $5\frac{1}{4}''$ high and $1\frac{3}{4}''$ wide. They may be painted or covered with paper representing the scenes in your plays. Some of the flats can be ' flown ', i.e. attached at the tops by strings to the wire-battens, and lowered into position when needed. (See Fig. 76.)

But most of the time it is more convenient to place them on the stage supported by a strut fixed at an angle to the back by cellotape. (See Fig. 77.)

For a set representing an interior—or ' box-set '—which would in the theatre be made up of a number of flats joined to one another you can use a long strip of cardboard. (See Fig. 78.)

Where you get the corners you can bend the cardboard. (See Fig. 79.)

Then doorways, windows, fireplaces, bookcases, etc. can be painted on or even cut out from the various wall-surfaces. (See Fig. 80.)

On the stage floor you can put blocks so that certain parts will be at a higher level than others, and these again may be made easily from cardboard.

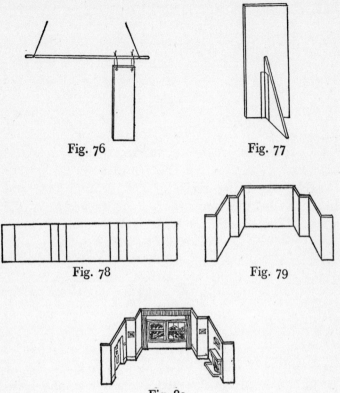

Fig. 76

Fig. 77

Fig. 78

Fig. 79

Fig. 80

If necessary steps and staircases can be built and any other items of furniture which you may want.

As well as the front curtains (measuring about 8″ square), which should be attached to the first batten and lowered to the stage floor between the proscenium arch and the $7\frac{3}{4}″$ by $2\frac{1}{8}″$ walls, you can also

147

have one or more sets of curtains, called ' traverses ', hung from a batten or battens to cut off back areas of the stage. These are often useful because a scene can be changed farther back while the play is still going on. Sometimes cloths or drops are used for this purpose instead of curtains.

You will also need borders to prevent the audience from seeing over the tops of your flats. These can be made of strips of dark material attached to the second, fifth and seventh battens —each strip being about 9″ long and 2″ deep and hung so that they are lower at the back than at the front. The ninth and tenth battens are probably best kept for ' back-drops ' or ' back-cloths '.

When not using a ' box-set ' the wings can be concealed by flats set at an angle on either side of the stage, and your traverse or traverses can help to do this as well.

Right at the back of the stage you may like to have a ' cyclorama '. This is a very large flat or cloth which curves forward at each end and gives the impression of sky and great distance much better than an ordinary flat cloth. This is easily made from cardboard bent round to form an arc. (See Fig. 81.) It can be flown from a batten or stood against the back wall.

Incidentally cut-out figures of actors and scenes can be bought at certain shops ; Benjamin Pollock Ltd., 44 Monmouth Street, London, W.C.2 sell

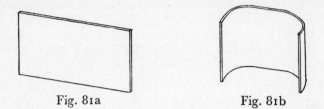

Fig. 81a   Fig. 81b

many of these 'Penny Plain and Twopence Coloured'
sheets.

The photograph facing page 109 shows the Modern
Theatre with a set representing the main deck and
part of the quarter-deck of a battleship of about
A.D. 1800.

LIGHTING

This can be a highly technical and very complicated business and there is no room here for going into much detail. In any case the lighting you may wish to have in your modern theatre is very much a matter of individual choice. It also depends on how much money you have and on your own knowledge of electricity. However, here are a few general remarks about it.

Lighting is of three main kinds : ' strip ' lighting which includes footlights, ' magazines ' battens, and ' groundrows ' ; individual lights which throw a wide beam called ' floods ' ; and individual lights which can throw a narrow beam called ' spots '.

The strip lights give general stage lighting, from below as footlights, from above or from the wings as battens, or concealed behind a rostrum or low piece of scenery such as a line of hills or a hedge to light up a back-drop or cyclorama. These are made up of a number of little torch bulbs in a row —sometimes each bulb being in a separate compartment. Behind the bulbs is a sheet of bright tin which acts as a reflector. The compartments can be covered with different coloured paper or gelatine to give different effects. These ' strips ' can be bought at certain shops and plugged into the mains. In your model they can be attached to the wire battens or placed on the stage concealed by a strip of scenery or even fixed in a trough cut away from the front of the stage floor.

The floods and spots, however, have to be connected to batteries or accumulators. Each one needs a little box of its own, with a reflector behind the bulb. The floods can be open at the front, but the spots need a front cover with a small hole cut in the centre. You can, of course, save a great deal of trouble by using very small torches—such as those made for fixing on a key ring to give a narrow beam of light for finding the ignition lock on the dashboard of a car. The floods will be most useful placed in the wings while the spots can be attached to the wires of the cat-walk or to the wire fixed across the second baffle.

If you wish to ' dim ' your lights you will need special devices called resistors.

Now, you can see that it's all a very difficult business. If you are determined to have lighting in your model as close as possible to the lighting of a real theatre, then you must be prepared to spend a great deal of time, a fair amount of money, and it might be a good idea to ask the advice of someone who knows a lot about electricity.

One final thing : each theatre in this book can be altered or added to. More decoration can be provided ; there is room under each stage for trap-doors ; you can put in more battens ; and the auditoriums can be enlarged to make complete theatre buildings.